Growing Together In Love

Growing Together In Love

God Known Through Family Life

ANNE BROYLES

UPPER ROOM BOOKS

GROWING TOGETHER IN LOVE
God Known Through Family Life

Scripture quotations not otherwise identified are from the New Revised Standard Version of the Bible, copyright © 1989 by the Division of Christian Education, National Council of the Churches of Christ in the United States of America, and are used by permission.

Scripture quotations designated RSV are from the Revised Standard Version of the Bible, copyrighted 1946, 1952, and © 1971 by the Division of Christian Education, National Council of the Churches of Christ in the United States of America, and are used by permission.

Scripture quotations designated TEV are from the *Good News Bible, The Bible in Today's English Version,* copyright by American Bible Society 1966, 1971, © 1976, and are used by permission.

Scripture quotations designated JB are from *The Jerusalem Bible,* copyright © 1966 by Darton, Longman & Todd, Ltd. and Doubleday & Company, Inc. Used by permission of the publishers.

Scripture quotations designated NIV are from the *Holy Bible, New International Version.* Copyright © 1973, 1978, 1984 International Bible Society. Used by permission of Zondervan Bible Publishers.

Antiphon from *God-With-Us: Resources for Prayer and Praise* by Sister Miriam Therese Winter. Copyright © 1978, 1982 Medical Mission Sisters. Used by permission.

Excerpt from "We've Come This Far by Faith" Copyright © 1963 by MANNA MUSIC, INC., 35255 Brooten Road, Pacific City, OR 97135. International Copyright Secured. All Rights Reserved. Used by permission.

Excerpt from "Through It All" Copyright © 1971 by MANNA MUSIC, INC., 35255 Brooten Road, Pacific City, OR 97135. International Copyright Secured. All Rights Reserved. Used by permission.

"Working for Justice" originally appeared as "Let There Be Light" in *Weavings,* Volume I, Number 2, November/December 1986.

Cover design: Nancy Hale
Cover photograph: Dave Reede/Westlight
First Printing: September 1993 (5)
ISBN: 0-8358-0687-1
Library of Congress Catalog Card Number: 93-60484

Printed in the United States of America

WITH LOVE AND THANKSGIVING TO

The family with whom I grew up:
    Wanda Sutherlin Broyles
    Frank Montgomery Broyles
    William Frank Broyles

The family with whom I continue to grow:
    Larry James Peacock
    Trinity Joy Peacock-Broyles
    Justus Simon Peacock-Broyles

Contents

Introduction

As a child, I dreamed of having eight children: one by birth, seven by adoption. Looking to the future, I meticulously thought out first and middle names for each child, knowing in my head which one was a redhead, which had brown eyes, which had the shy smile. I played out this fantasy with my dolls, drew it in pictures, wrote it down on each Sunday's attendance registration card at church. The names had deep literary allusions; they represented all four of the March sisters, plus characters from many of my other favorite books.

I loved my future children. I saw myself as a *Cheaper by the Dozen* mom, active as mother and career woman. I worked in the church nursery, cared for the youngest ones at vacation Bible school, and baby-sat for a variety of families. Photographs from that time most frequently show me with a baby on one hip. From my earliest years, I felt called to motherhood.

By late high school, I also felt called to ministry. Even before I knew ministry's demands of long hours and emotional self-giving, I realized that it would not be easy to be a full-time minister and mother to eight children. I scaled my vision down numerically but assumed I would be the active, enthusiastic mom of my dreams: always available to her children, offering creative art projects, introducing them to great literature, spending time outdoors sharing God's good creation.

I met my husband in seminary. As we sat on a couch at a Valentine's Day party, listening to the rain flood down on the streets of Evanston, we discovered that we both loved to travel. We both had returned recently from long trips to Europe. Larry had spent two years as an intern minister in Manchester, England; I was just two months back in the States after seven months backpacking around Western Europe. During that first conversation, our talk was of adventure and wanderlust—not of diapers and Dr. Seuss. But it soon became apparent that we both felt called to parenting.

It was five and a half years before our first child was born. Larry and I prepared for her birth over those years just as we prepared for our ministry careers by going to seminary, serving intern situations, and talking to those already serving as ministers. We felt strongly that parenting required more preparation and forethought than did our careers; one can always change careers, but one cannot easily walk away from the child one has birthed.

To become pregnant obviously does not require the conscious decision-making process that Larry and I underwent. Call us compulsive or crazy, but we spent the first six months of the year 1980 in personal "research" and soul-searching to evaluate whether we were ready to include a child in our relationship and lifestyle. The book *Ourselves and Our Children* served as an invaluable resource as I reflected on my childhood dreams of mothering and wondered if they could become reality:

> Do I want to have children at all? When do I want
> to have them? Answering these questions means
> dealing with ill-defined and unquantifiable factors

such as self-image, life goals, romantic ideals, spiritual beliefs and personal needs and expectations. Add to that our parents' dreams for us, society's program for us, our friends' ideas about us, and our own hidden agenda for ourselves. . . .

My initial reactions to my readings were varied. My attitude would vacillate between "I'm ready!" and "Are you kidding?" I would fantasize about the joy of holding my newborn, then see a picture of a toddler pulling books from a shelf. "Am I ready for all the changes my well-ordered life would have to take?" My life would certainly change if I became a mother.

I felt drawn to parenting because I felt I would be a good mother. I believed that the world needs children who are educated to be loving global citizens, and I was brash enough to think I could help raise such kids. The more I read and talked to other parents, the more certain I became that parenting could be an avenue of service to God, a way to share life with another and to give to the world as well.

I did not need to have children in order to be fulfilled. I was happy with my life as a woman, a wife, and a minister. Still I increasingly felt called by God to care for God's children; not just generally, but specifically as a mother and primary caregiver. Not everyone is called to be a physician or concert pianist or missionary to Latin America, and not everyone is called to be a parent. Many people have children without ever feeling such a calling. These people manage to raise their children without the sense that it is God who has charged them to provide a home for their daughters and sons.

For me, parenting has been an extension of my faith in Jesus Christ. This is not to say that if I were not Christian I could not be a good parent; it is an acknowledgment of my "home base," the reality from which I view the world and find my place in it. The same Jesus who asked his disciples to bring small children to him wishes only the best for all the earth's children. The same Jesus who said, "Whoever receives one such child in my name receives me" (Mark 9:37), wants every child to grow up feeling secure and loved.

When our children were born, I was not surprised to discover that I could love them deeply. My years of experience as a baby-sitter and nanny had showed me that I could connect well with youngsters. I have not been surprised to discover that I can be a good mother. I have realized many aspects of my childhood's mothering fantasies in raising our children. The big surprise for me has been that, as I have tried to help my children discover the power of God in this world, I too have grown, changed, and learned of God in new and mysterious ways.

Forgiveness, honesty, love, redemption—what better place to act out these aspects of the Christian faith than with those whom we share daily life? This book is an attempt to share with you how God has become more real to me through the simple activities of family life: mealtimes, camping trips, family squabbles, and the many other rituals we develop as we act out our faith. You will doubtless remember stories from your own family life which may illustrate similar or different biblical principles.

Every family has its times of knowing and showing God's love as it works through human love. I have found a closer relationship to God through my inner circle of relationship with

is for church family as much as for individual families

Larry, Trinity, and Justus. My prayer for you is that whether you are single or married, with or without children, you will find community in which you can experience the power of God.

I encourage you to try some of the rituals and activities listed for each chapter at the end of this book. I pray that you and your loved ones will find ever-new ways of relating to the One who has given us families as a place to grow together in love.

ANNE BROYLES
October 1992

Cocreators with God

As I gave birth to Trinity, our firstborn child, I felt directly connected to the creative power of God. I was strongly conscious of God's presence as I labored to bring Trinity's body down the birth canal toward the light of life. When her body finally emerged, vernix-covered and slippery, thanksgiving flooded over me. If I had needed proof of the existence of God, this seven-pound, fourteen-ounce wonder was enough.

The miracle of life amazed me—that a human being could quietly grow inside of me for nine months and then (with quite a bit of effort on both our parts) emerge perfect and whole. I felt strong and powerful, a cocreator with God. My self-image altered. *I am one who gives birth,* I thought to myself. *The Creator God is in me, empowering and powerful.* Giving life was all that mattered. The pain I had endured so recently was gone, transitory; the power of life was eternal.

I had been amazed by the primacy of birth. That basic urge to push came from across centuries of womanhood, not just from within me. I felt connected to all of life, but especially to all women who had ever given birth—prehistoric cavewomen, Anazazi cliff dwellers, French marquises—mothers in all times and places.

I thought of the creative God who looked upon the earth, the seas, the creatures and plants and saw that "it was very good." I gazed upon my newborn daughter and knew without a doubt that she also was one of God's good creations. Trinity was *of God* as much as she was made of the melding of Larry's and my genes. And with God's help, my husband and I would nurture Trinity as she grew.

If I thought I had to be all and everything for my children, I could not face the task. I am strengthened by the knowledge that God holds both children and parents in the palm of God's mighty hand. I rely on God for wisdom and strength in all I do, especially as a parent. At times I need to pray for my children and can only place them in God's hands. I cannot be with them every minute of their lives to assure their physical, spiritual, and emotional safety. At times I need to pray that I will have God's spirit in *me* as I relate to my family members and make decisions that affect their lives.

Moses was God's partner as he led the Hebrew people from slavery to the Promised Land. Esther realized that it was for "such a time as this" that she was born; the risks she took were taken in partnership with God. Throughout the Bible, we have examples of ordinary people who did extraordinary things because they were attuned to the spirit of the living God at work in their lives.

Parenting may not seem like such an extraordinary activity; after all, millions of people are parents. However, when we stop and take stock of the incredible gift God entrusts to us when we are given children, we realize that parenting is much more than conceiving and giving birth to a child or going through the adoption process. Parenting is relationship, intimacy, challenge, risk. Becoming a parent opens us to the possibility of change, for who can stay the same after giving one's heart to a child?

16

Parenting is a lifelong education in what it means to be human. I may present myself to the public as calm, capable, patient, and all the good things I want to be; but in my most intimate relationships with husband and children, I expose my true self. I am not always calm or capable or patient. I don't always say or do the loving thing. However, I am loved in spite of my weaknesses and, wonder of wonders, my family calls forth from me a depth of love and caring that I never knew possible. Yes, I am sometimes a grouch, considering only my own needs and unmindful of the needs of others. But I am also at times wonderfully accepting of my family members and perceptive of their needs.

In our family, we try to be sensitive to the fact that at any given time at least one of us may be a) tired, b) under stress, c) going through an emotionally trying time, or d) all of the above. Whether it's a deadline for a book report or for a book manuscript, a cold or the flu, a misunderstanding with a best friend, or recovery from a slumber party, we are not always at our best. *Larry* (or Anne or Trinity or Justus) *has had a hard day*, we realize, *and so we need to be gentle with him or her*. We know that God is merciful to us, so we likewise try to show mercy to one another.

We understand that being in a family means being in partnership. This involves sharing the work so there's time to play together, being flexible in order to meet one another's needs, and understanding that each of us takes turns being needy and providing for the needs of others. One day I called home to say that I was late returning from a meeting and was caught in freeway traffic. I told Trinity, who had answered the phone, to tell her dad that I would not be home for dinner until six. "That's okay," my nine-year-old replied, "Dad came home sick from work, so Justus and I are fixing dinner. We'll take care of everything."

When I drove into the driveway, tired from a long day's work and the tensions of a backed-up freeway, my two children ran out to meet me with aprons on. "Your restaurant is ready!" they cried. "Go wash up and come to eat."

The table was set as if for a banquet: Guatemalan weaving for decoration, several sizes and shape of candlesticks, and our special crystal goblets for drinks. Once Larry and I were seated, our servers (aprons off) came around with the printed-in-pencil menu: freshly-baked cornbread with or without honey butter, bagel with cream cheese, bagel with peanut butter and jelly, garlic bagel, fruit plate, sparkling cider or water, and two kinds of Girl Scout cookies for dessert. Perhaps not the most balanced meal but prepared and served with love. This "love feast" was for me proof that by raising our children mindful of *their* needs, they were growing to be concerned about the needs of others as well.

We are growing together, parents and children; we are partners in learning. We have much to learn in life. As adults, we often take for granted the immense effort a developing child invests in "learning the ropes." Children pick up much practical knowledge by watching, listening, and trying out new ideas on their own. They grow even more quickly when a parent takes the time to share knowledge (and ignorance) with them along the way.

I had never given much thought to the mechanics of eating an ice cream cone, for instance, until Trinity was a toddler. Certain "pointers" from an old ice-cream-eating pro then seemed to be in order: 1) the top part of the ice cream must be well-licked to prevent dripping (with an occasional maintenance lick-all-over to avert disaster); 2) in hot weather, little mouths need to take bites as well as licks; and 3) the ice cream itself should be eaten first, as a bite from the bottom of the cone could endanger the entire arrangement.

Now this knowledge may not appear to be of earthshaking importance. A trip to Baskin-Robbins or Dairy Queen is not necessarily an intellectual exercise. Yet day after day, no matter what the age of the child, we have countless opportunities (often mundane) for learning as partners.

Learning with one's child is not simply a matter of drawing from one's own experience and then imparting gifts of wisdom. It is a sharing, a growing together. To explain seemingly simple things (let alone things that are over my head) I use myself, my life, my society, and my faith. The questions come not only from an inquiring child's mind but also from my inner self:

- Am I approaching this in the spirit of Jesus Christ?
- Why do I think it is important to teach about this? What does this say about who I am and what I believe?

I don't lie awake at night pondering these pressing issues. Rather, at odd moments a question will pop into my head as I drive down Pacific Coast Highway or stand in the grocery line.

My children keep me on my toes with new questions that continually arise. "Why?" is not a stage; it is a way of life. Out of the blue, Justus will ask, "Do you think it took God a long time to decide to destroy the earth with a flood?" Or Trinity may ask, "How do radio waves travel?" I often reply, "What do *you* think?" This gives them the chance to figure it out for themselves. It also gives me an extra minute to see if I can answer a particular question or must plead ignorance!

My children's responses are often more perceptive than mine, though not always traditionally "correct." If my children ask a question for which I don't have a ready answer (and as they get older, I seem to have fewer ready answers), I can give them one of two gifts: First, the reply "I don't know" imparts the gift of saying "Even parents don't know everything. Every human being has more to learn." Second, if I say "Since I don't know, perhaps you and I can find out the answer together," then I share with them the gift of learning in partnership.

Partner-learning means that I, too, am learning in my children's presence. I may be able to explain the chronology of Paul's travels, but my children challenge me to look deeper into the mind and soul of Paul himself. I can teach my children how to use a computer, but their questions help me marvel at the fact that human creativity spawned a new generation of machinery and knowledge.

We learn together. We teach one another. We grow as partners in learning. And I, despite much academic experience, am as much learner as teacher, grateful for the wisdom that comes from the experience and insight of my children.

Because we value our children as full human beings with much to teach us, Larry and I early on instituted "family meetings" as a way to resolve conflicts and squabbles. Having been trained by Kathleen and James McGinnis in *Parenting for Peace and Justice*, we had seen the success of family meetings in the lives of other families.

Agenda for these meetings comes from our life experience together. Any one of us can call a family meeting in order to discuss issues as varied as whether a sibling trade of Playmobil toys is null and void, whether Justus should clean up his dog's droppings in the yard more frequently, and whether Trinity can buy a Ninja Turtle toy when our household does not allow weapons.

We take turns chairing the meeting and try to listen to one another's feelings so that we can come to consensus on the issues. After everyone has shared his or her perceptions on a given issue, we usually come to agreement on a solution that works for all of us.

I'm sure some people have been taken aback by the fact that we have never spanked our children. Our commitment as peacemakers makes no sense to us if we use force against anyone, including our children. Hitting a child to teach that hitting another child was wrong seems inconsistent. We have always tried to reason with our children and to help them discover ways they might deal with a particular situation. Certainly, in their early years, spanking might have proved more initially beneficial; it is not easy to reason with a two-year-old. Yet we have seen our children grow in self-control because they have learned to self-discipline rather than fear a parent's punishment.

When discipline is in order, we often let the child choose the appropriate consequence. They are much harder on themselves than we would be. "Take all my Playmobil away for a year," Justus may say. "That's a pretty harsh consequence for throwing a tantrum," we may respond. "Shall we put it away for a week?"

We as parents have ultimate authority in our family. Many times we have to make "executive decisions" to deal with matters of health and safety. As far as possible, however, we try to involve our children in the decision-making process so that they are learning to be responsible for their own lives and to be faithful to who God has called them to be.

> *Children, it is your Christian duty to obey your parents, for this is the right thing to do. "Respect your father and mother" is the first commandment that has a promise added: "so that all may go well with you, and you may live a long time in the land."*
>
> *Parents, do not treat your children in such a way as to make them angry. Instead, raise them with Christian discipline and instruction.*
>
> —Ephesians 6:1-4, TEV

Because Larry, Trinity, Justus, and I respect one another and see our family working as a team under God's purposes, we learn together about God and how God is working in our life and world. Together we learn and grow toward wholeness as cocreators with one another and with God.

Known by God

*L*ooking out at the playground, I saw her. Thirty children romped around, running this way and that as they played a variety of games. But I could instantly pick out the toss of my daughter's head as she surveyed the possibilities for play. I was so familiar with her way of standing, her tennis shoe scuffing the ground, her fingers slipping into her mouth—an insecure moment was coming upon her. From a distance, I felt what *she* felt.

I looked to see who might play with Trinity. What child would affirm her, welcome her, accept her? Part of me wanted to run to her to offer hugs and an "I love you." The other (wiser) part of me knew that she needed to work out the dynamics of being the new kid at nursery school for herself.

My love was there to boost Trinity from a distance, undergirding her when she felt unsure of herself. My love was there to listen to how her day had been and to reassure her about the days to come. On some level, she felt my love even as she stood with her fingers in her mouth, her shoe drawing circles in the sand.

I thought of God's long-distance, undergirding love inside each of us. Even as I know my daughter in such an intimate way, God knows each of us more deeply. Even as I guessed Trinity's thoughts, the Almighty keenly knows what we are thinking.

Even as I wished all the best for my child, our gracious God gives the best to all children.

I knew her so well, yet my knowing and my loving were only a fraction of the way each human being is known and loved by the One who created us and gave us life. We are known by God as no other can know us. We are loved as only God can love. We belong to God.

> *For thou didst form my inward parts,*
> *thou didst knit me together in my mother's womb.*
> *I praise thee, for thou art fearful and wonderful.*
> *Wonderful are thy works!*
> *Thou knowest me right well.*
>
> —Psalm 139:13-14, RSV

One of the mysteries of the parent-child relationship is that no matter how well we know our children, as parents, we also realize that there are depths in their interior lives that we will never begin to know. In so many ways, Trinity is like me. Justus is like me in other ways. Yet, again and again I am amazed at how they respond to particular situations. I am reminded constantly that they are unique persons with only some similarities to who *I* am.

As much as a son or daughter may be like a mother or father, he or she is ever so much more like God. For Christians, part of the parents' job is to nourish that Godlikeness in their children. As we gaze lovingly at our children, we can pray with Paul who wrote to the church at Ephesus:

24

For this reason I fall on my knees before [God], from whom every family in heaven and on earth receives its true name. I ask God from the wealth of [God's] glory to give you power through [God's] Spirit to be strong in your inner selves, and I pray that Christ will make his home in your hearts through faith. I pray that you may have your roots and foundation in love, so that you, together with all God's people, may have the power to understand how broad and long, how high and deep, is Christ's love. Yes, may you come to know [Christ's] love—although it can never be fully known—and so be completely filled with the very nature of God.

—Ephesians 3:14-19, TEV

How do we help our children make Christ's home in their hearts through faith? What can we do to nurture them so that they grow in Godlikeness? Even though each living being will come to God in a unique way, much of faith comes through tradition. Justus and Trinity are growing up knowing that both sets of grandparents and many of their great-grandparents were people of faith. Going to church is part of life. Prayer is a given. At family gatherings, folks feel free to talk about faith issues and to share about the life of their particular congregation of faith.

Paul wrote to Timothy, "I am reminded of your sincere faith, a faith that lived first in your grandmother Lois and your mother Eunice and now, I am sure, lives in you" (2 Tim. 1:5).

My Grandma Verna taught me much about faith. Her total reliance on the Bible and frequent quoting of important verses surrounded me with a security that God was present and accounted for, acting in the world. We didn't have theological discussions, but I took in Grandma Verna's faith by osmosis, knowing how to be attentive to her faith-sharing even as I paid attention to her teaching me how to play pinochle and to make her famous "Peanut Butter Goop."

My years as a seminary student and local church pastor cause me to encourage Trinity and Justus to look at life theologically, applying the Bible to specific situations in their lives. However, whatever I seek to impart cannot be more important than the quiet sense of godliness I received by spending time in Grandma Verna's presence.

Recently, Justus came to me with a complaint. "Let's go in the meditation garden and talk," I said, knowing that the peacefulness of that place would have its own calming effect. Trinity had had a friend, Georgia, over to spend the night. Since Georgia's brother, Jules, is Justus's good friend, I suggested that both of the children spend the next night.

"It's not fair," Justus began. (I have to confess that those three words cause my stomach to tighten in resistance to what I am about to hear; I have to *work* at being open to my child's feelings.) "It's not fair that Trinity gets to have Georgia over two nights when I only get to have my friend for one night."

"How many nights did you want Jules to stay?"

"One," Justus replied. "One's enough."

"So why does it matter that Trinity's friend stays two nights?"

"Because it's not *fair* ! Georgia should have to go home."

I sat quietly for a moment, watching a hummingbird dart in and out of the flowering jasmine that covers our fence. Rather than making my own editorial comments, I decided to use one of Jesus' methods of teaching.

"Do you know the story of the employer who needed workers?" I asked. "He went out to the streets and hired some people early in the morning, promising to pay them twenty dollars to work in his vineyard. Then, at other times in the day, he went out and hired more workers, each time sending them out to work in his vineyard. He hired the last group just a short time before quitting time."

Justus looked at me intently. "And . . . ?"

"When it was time to quit work, all the workers came back to receive their paychecks. First, the employer paid twenty dollars each to those who had worked just a short time. Then he paid the same amount to those hired at three o'clock, at noon, and at nine o'clock."

Justus waited expectantly for the punchline.

"When the employer called up those who had worked hard all day long in the hot sun, how much do you think *they* got paid?"

"Fifty dollars? Sixty?" Justus ventured.

"Those who were hired early and worked all day were paid the same as all the rest: twenty dollars." I watched his face grow incredulous.

"But that's not *fair!*" he said, wondering what this story was all about.

"That's exactly what those first-hired workers said. They complained to the employer: "That's not fair!" The employer reminded them that he had paid them exactly what he had promised to pay and that it was his choice what to pay the others."

We sat, leaning against each other, silent for a moment.

"I think Jesus told this story to say that God gives everybody what they need, even though we sometimes think we should get more." This text exegesis was not seminary quality, perhaps, but I thought it would help to make a point.

We sat quietly a while longer, then Justus got up.

"I guess it's okay for Georgia to stay," he said, then went back into the house, no longer angry.

Part of my job as Justus's mother is to help him know who he is and grow to be a responsible adult. I am also called to help him know *whose* he is. When I take time to share stories from the Christian faith, I am giving Justus tools to deal with life's complexities. Modern survival requires knowledge, common sense, and faith. I have to be careful not to preach at him or to concentrate so hard on trying to make my point that I forget to listen to *his* perspective. I am continually amazed at how, when I bring a faith perspective to an everyday conflict or dilemma, things sort themselves out fairly smoothly.

The tables can turn, of course. As Trinity and Justus grow in faith, at times they will remind *me* that a particular problem I'm having may have a God-answer. I have to be ready to learn from them and their unique perspectives.

When Trinity was five or six, she began to seriously question the power of God. At first Larry and I were taken aback by her vehement statements of "I don't believe in God!" But we tried to let her talk through her feelings rather than judge her for her faith struggle.

"So you don't believe in God," Larry said casually one night as they sat together on the couch. I washed dishes in the kitchen nearby, listening in.

"No," Trinity responded in a definite tone of voice.

"Lots of people don't believe in God."

This surprised her. Her life was so church-related that most of her circle of friends and acquaintances were fairly religious.

"What do they believe in?"

"Some people don't believe in anything."

"They don't!" There was total amazement in Trinity's voice. "So who made the world, then?"

"Some people have a scientific explanation for the creation of the world that doesn't need someone like God to do the creating."

"Who do they think takes care of the world?"

"I don't think they worry about someone taking care of the world."

"Are they scared, not having God?"

"You'd have to ask them." Larry was playing this cool. "Why don't *you* believe in God?"

"Well, a lot of bad things happen to people, and I think God shouldn't let bad things happen."

"It bothers me too that bad things happen," Larry replied. "I sometimes wonder why God doesn't stop hurt and war and suffering."

I couldn't keep silent any longer. "Sometimes, Trinity, I talk to God about the bad things and how sad I feel when I hear about hurting people."

"Does God listen?"

"It feels to me like God listens." I dried my hands and went to join my husband and daughter.

"Does God get mad when you talk about that?" We cuddled close together on the couch.

"No. God just listens." Larry and I smiled at each other.

"Hey Dad! Do you ever talk like that to God?"

"Sure," Larry replied, stroking her hair. "I talk to God about lots of things. God listens and understands."

"I didn't think it was okay to talk to God like that. I thought I just had to stop believing in God." Trinity shook her head. This was hard to believe.

"Most people have some times in their lives when they have serious questions for God," I said. "There are times when it *is* hard to believe in God because it just seems too incredible that God can love us so much even when we botch things—like starting wars and hurting each other."

"Did you ever have times of not believing?" Trinity's eyes were big as she looked from one parent to the other.

We both nodded our heads.

"Sure," Larry responded. "But God didn't give up on me. And the more I thought things through, the more I realized that this life doesn't make sense *without God*."

"Me too," Trinity said, yawning. "I guess I'll just have to give God time to help me understand."

My daughter went on to bed that night with an expanded vision of God. Larry and I had a long talk about whether we handled her questions appropriately or not. (The first child is often the guinea pig for new parents as they come face to face with issues for which they feel unprepared.)

Several years later, Trinity does believe in God and continues to grow in faith despite occasional questions she may have concerning theological dilemmas. And I rest secure knowing that God knows and loves her, accepts her questioning, affirms her seeking, and embraces her believing.

As Trinity's mother, I affirm what Paul said to the church at Philippi:

I am confident of this, that the one who began a good work among you will bring it to completion by the day of Jesus Christ. It is right for me to think this way about all of you, because you hold me in your heart, for all of you share in God's grace with me.

—Philippians 1:6-7

Appreciating God's Good Gifts

*E*very morning, as soon as the alarm clock summons me from the pleasure of sleep, I take a walk. No matter where I am, I find that even if my mind is hardly awake, my feet can navigate me into consciousness. It is not just alertness I desire, but also gratitude. Whether I am walking in the Malibu canyon where I live or out in the desert of Tucson or along a strange city street, a few minutes into my walk, I find myself flooded with a profound sense of thankfulness.

Usually, the beauty of the early morning stillness reminds me of God's gifts, and I remember not only the natural world that surrounds me but all those many things for which I am thankful. I want my children to grow up with this pervasive thankfulness, as well, remembering that "every good gift and every perfect present comes from heaven" (James 1:17, TEV). For this reason our family takes specific times each day to "give thanks to the God of heaven, for [God's] steadfast love endures forever" (Psalm 136:26).

When I wake my children in the morning, I often say, "This is the day God has made. Let's rejoice and be glad in it," or "Another beautiful day from God, so it will be a good day." On birthdays, Trinity and Justus receive a wake-up call with the Spanish song "Las Mañanitas" that, loosely translated, says:

> This is the morning song that King David sang
> But it isn't as pretty as the one we sing here.
> Awake, my love, awake.
> Look! The dawn already comes
> And the bird sings.
> The moon has already gone down.

My children do not understand all the words to this song but they know it is special and have heard it as many times as they have celebrated birthdays. Music transcends the barriers of language and reaches to that place deep in our hearts where we understand what is truly important.

Little by little, as we and our children have grown and changed, we have added small prayer rituals to our daily lives. These have encouraged us to live thankfully. It would not have worked to say one day, "We are going to incorporate morning prayer, mealtime graces, a family day book, and a nighttime song to what we do each day." Each ritual has become part of us one at a time. These rituals feel comfortable and are very much part of our family.

Eleven years ago, Larry began a wonderful discipline that provides a daily reminder of who we are, where we have been, and how we have been blessed in our everyday lives. He took two three-ring notebooks and filled them both with enough paper for each day of six months of the year. One notebook documents January to June; the other contains July through December. At the top of each blank sheet of paper, Larry wrote the date. Certain days note historical events (Martin Luther King's birthday, the day of Gandhi's death, International Women's Day). Many pages have a special quote or Bible verse.

These two simple notebooks hold the record of our family's life since 1981. Every morning at breakfast, Larry records what the previous day was like for our family. Was there a soccer game? a hard test? Did we do something exciting? Was someone sick? Each day, Larry not only records the preceding day's activities, but he reads aloud what our family's life included on the current day in years gone by.

A typical day, viewed over the years, might record Justus's learning to say the word *frog* in 1985, Trinity's starting violin lessons in 1986, Larry's leading a retreat in 1988, and my flying to Nashville in 1990. Not all days contain earthshaking or memorable events, but all days illustrate how blessed we have been as we have lived through these past years.

Some entries bring laughter. "Oh, I remember *that!*" Other days remind us of sad events, people we miss, places that are no longer part of our lives. However, we cannot help but give thanks for those people, places, and events that have revealed God to us.

Patterns also become apparent. Almost every year, shortly after Christmas and Easter, at least someone in our family is sick, confirming our suspicion that church holy days are hard work for clergy families. We often travel or go camping or have friends over on the same days each year. And although we don't take much time to analyze the how and why of those patterns, we realize that our life is cyclical and that "for everything there is a season" (Eccles. 3:1).

Larry first gave this family date book to the family as his "Jesus Gift" on Christmas. It is an important part of our life together, and I am thankful to Larry for his long-term dedication to this family history project.

The "Jesus Gift" is a clear reminder of what Christmas is all about. No matter what other gifts we may choose to make or buy for one another at Christmas, we strive to give one gift that is designed to bring the other person closer to God.

Though this gift may not cost the giver a penny, it is often more time-consuming in careful deliberation of what to give and its enactment. One year, Larry gave me a small stand-up plastic frame, promising to put a different quote in it each week to inspire me in my faith. Another year, I spent more hours than I care to remember sewing matching satin chasubles in jewel colors for Larry and myself. We may give time away at a retreat center or a writing week. As the children grow, they will find their own ways of choosing appropriate Jesus Gifts.

Another Christmas ritual that helps us to concentrate on Jesus' birth (and not just on how many gifts each of us has piled up under the tree) is our "Welcome, Jesus!" time. When we first awaken on Christmas morning, we come as a family into the living room. Before we check out the goodies under the tree, we process around the house saying "Welcome, Jesus!" to each and every representation of the baby Jesus that decorates our home. This procession continues for some time, as we have collected nativity sets from around the world and also decorate the walls of several rooms with Christmas memorabilia. We acknowledge each carved figure, painting, or stuffed baby, then end our procession at the Advent candle on the dining room table. After lighting the four candles of pink and purple, we light the Jesus candle and sing our Advent song. Then, (finally!) we are ready to look at the tree and its bounty.

Christmas is one of many special "red plate days." A dear friend gave us a "You are special today" red plate which we have used at meals for special occasions. The person celebrating a birthday or baptism anniversary eats off the red plate. Anniversaries of our baptism remind us of our initiation into the "household of faith" so that we can truly "remember our baptism and be thankful." Easter is also an important holiday at our house. In addition to the traditional Easter baskets and dyed eggs, we celebrate Easter with our own special rituals and Christian decorations for our home. By having an assortment of "red plate days" when we remember God acting in human history, we are called again and again to thankfulness.

Mealtime graces give us a moment to quiet and center ourselves before plunging into the meal. Breakfast grace is accompanied by simple sign language gestures:

> Loving Jesus, be our holy guest,
> Our morning joy, our evening rest.
> And with this food to us impart
> Justice and peace to every heart.

We use a variety of graces for lunch and dinner and take turns choosing which grace to use at a particular meal. We say some graces and sing some. Most frequently we choose a time of silence—a gift from our sabbatical year spent among Quakers at Pendle Hill. So that our guests can join us, we have the words to each grace written out on a three-inch by five-inch card. A pencil stuck in a plaster of Paris holder with a clothespin on the top makes it easy to clamp the appropriate grace for all to see.

For many families, bedtime is also a traditional time for thanksgiving. When our children were young, we sat with each of them to go over the "goods, bads, happys, sads" of the day that was ending. We brought all of the day's experiences to God, knowing that every emotion was understood and blessed. Trinity and Justus now say their own prayers when the light is turned out, but we continue to sing our nighttime song collectively. It is a haunting melody from a Benedictine monastery Larry likes to visit:

> Keep us, God, as we wake.
> Guard us as we sleep.
> So may we wake in Christ
> And take our rest in peace.

Whether one of us is traveling, spending the night with a friend, or coming home late, we know that the song will be sung. I have sung this melody to myself while going to sleep in a hotel room thousands of miles away from my family and have slept securely, feeling close to my husband and children. I have smiled broadly as I lay in my sleeping bag in our tent, singing in quartet with my family at a national park campsite. Our bedtime song goes wherever we go.

There are other less-ritualized times to say thank-you to God. Whenever we land safely while on an airplane flight or pull into our driveway after a trip, we say thank-you to God for safe travel. We do not always remember to acknowledge God's role in our lives, of course; many times we are too wrapped up in the tasks of the moment to give thanks for what has happened. However, we remember Jesus' words to the Samaritan woman at the well;

"If you only knew what God gives" (John 4:10, TEV). When we are in touch with the power of God in our lives, we connect with "a spring of water gushing up to eternal life" (John 4:14).

Justus and Trinity do not spend all their time saying prayers. Whether or not they are conscious of *how* God is working in their lives, however, my children realize that God *is* the center of their lives, undergirding them at all moments.

Just as we recognize God's good gifts to us, we try to be conscious of how we spend and give away the gifts of money and time. Because Larry and I decided that we wanted to spend as much time as possible with our children while they were young, we have arranged for a combined workload of one and a quarter positions. It is wonderful to have this increased family time. The downside of this arrangement is that sometimes our salary doesn't stretch very far after we tithe ten percent to the church and strive to give another twenty percent to other groups and causes.

When we need to make big financial decisions, we try to include the children as much as possible. We want them to know the choices we have—where to make a donation, how to shop with socially responsible criteria, why we choose to boycott certain products, why we shop at thrift stores, and why we continue to drive our 1981 Honda Civic with its 130,000 miles.

One of the hard parts of living in Malibu (a community that is more than, but also includes, a rich and famous image) is that just about everyone we know has more material resources than we. Larry and I try to guide our family to keep this in perspective, however, since we have more money than most people in the world. Living in an environment of multimillion-dollar homes, stretch limousines, housekeepers, gardeners, and nannies, we occasionally have to remind ourselves that these items are luxuries, *not necessities*. While we cannot afford what many in Malibu take for granted, we also have to be careful that we do not fall into the "poor us" syndrome. We have a lovely parsonage, plenty to eat, enough clothes. Because we try to live simply in many ways, we are able to feed six pets and always take a low-cost but exciting summer vacation. Violin lessons, sports activities, and Spanish classes fit into our budget. And we have the satisfaction of knowing that thirty percent of our income reaches beyond our home to people in need throughout the world.

As a parent, I want to prepare my children to make the day-to-day decisions, which will include financial spending. We may talk about how a designated amount could be spent for a meal out, a video rental and pizza, a night of camping, a donation to the homeless, or be set aside for a long-term goal. I don't want Justus or Trinity to feel that we don't have enough; I do want them to realize that expenditures are choices about values and lifestyle.

So far, both children have amazed us by their practicality. One time, for instance, I realized that Trinity had an important violin recital coming up.

"Trinity, maybe we should go buy some fabric and make a new dress for your recital."

"Why?"

"Well, a recital is always special, and sometimes it's nice to have a special dress for the occasion."

"Mom," Trinity said in a patient voice, "I have dresses that are good enough. We don't need to spend money on something new. There are a lot of other places for the money to go."

I didn't argue with that logic, but I also try to be sensitive to those times when either child may ask for something that may *not* be completely practical or necessary but is, at that time, important to their sense of self-esteem. Little splurges make life fun. Although we have tried to live simply, we also know that life is to be celebrated. Sometimes a carton of ice cream or a trip to the movies is important to family life.

We know ourselves to be richly blessed, and we realize that it is not just in our finances that we give to the world. We strive to live in love, giving of our time in ways that reach beyond our material resources. As Paul reminds us,

> *Remember that the person who plants few seeds will have a small crop; the one who plants many seeds will have a large crop. Each one should give, then, as he has decided, not with regret or out of a sense of duty; for God loves the one who gives gladly. And God is able to give you more than you need, so that you will always have all you need for yourselves and more than enough for every good cause. As the scripture says, "[God] gives generously to the needy; God's kindness lasts forever."*
>
> *And God, who supplies seed for the sower and bread to eat, will also supply you with all the seed you need and will make it grow and produce a rich harvest from your generosity. [God] will always make you rich enough to be generous at all times, so that many will thank God for your gifts which they receive from us. For this service you perform not only meets the needs of God's people, but also produces an outpouring of gratitude to God. And because of the proof which this*

service of yours brings, many will give glory to God for your loyalty to the gospel of Christ, which you profess, and for your generosity in sharing with them and everyone else. And so with deep affection they will pray for you because of the extraordinary grace God has shown you. Let us thank God for [this] priceless gift!

—2 Corinthians 9:6-15, TEV

The Power of Prayer

I hate first grade! I want to go back to kindergarten," Justus yelled, stomping into his room. My husband, Larry, and I looked at each other in surprise. Was this the same child who had loved kindergarten? who had worked joyfully all summer learning the basics of reading?

Justus had a difficult time making the transition to first grade at Malibu Park School. As we dealt with his negative feelings, however, we were able to know the power of God in a new way and grow even closer as a family.

The first days of school are always exciting—new class, new teacher, new classmates. For first-graders at our local public school, there was also a transition to a different building and playground setting. Justus's older sister, Trinity, had made the transition without comment. For Justus, though, too many changes were coming at him too fast. Not only were his two best friends in different classrooms, but first grade offered a more structured environment.

"Tell me about your day at school," I would ask, trying to discover what was making him so angry and belligerent.

"Well, we start on the playground and the bell rings and we have to go inside. Then the bell rings, and we have to go outside. Then the bell rings, and we have to go inside again. That's all we do—go in and out when the bell tells us to."

"But what different sorts of things do you do when you're in the classroom?"

"It doesn't matter because the bell always interrupts me, and I never get to finish any project I'm working on." The structure of first grade (symbolized by the bells) was obviously a sore point for this barely six-year-old child. Careful and methodical once he was involved in a project, Justus was a boy who could spend hours in his room looking at books, doing puzzles, or creating artwork. Now he saw the class structure as intruding on his need to complete each project before going on to the next.

When I spoke to the teacher about Justus's unhappiness, she said, "I'm glad you came in because I really need to talk to *you* about the way Justus is behaving in class. He is quite disruptive, finding small ways to interrupt the class by kicking his desk or crumpling up paper. When he does writing, he presses the pencil so hard, the paper rips as he scribbles." She looked at me carefully. "He's a very angry little boy."

I was glad that I had known this teacher years before when her son attended an afterschool program at our church. I trusted her and knew she had Justus's best interests at heart. Her only experience of Justus, however, was these first few days in the first grade classroom.

"Maybe it would be better for Justus to go back to kindergarten."

I protested. "But he's already reading and doing basic math."

"But maybe he isn't ready socially."

I felt certain that if we could help Justus adjust to a more structured environment, he could succeed at first grade this time around.

Justus continued to act out at school and at home. After he was sent home one day for disrupting the class while a substitute was in charge, the assistant principal suggested an alternative school. There Justus would learn in a less-structured environment. We presented this option to our son, truthfully telling him that the forty-minute, one-way commute to the alternative school would change things.

"You have two good options, Justus. At the alternative school, there wouldn't be any bells, and you could learn at your own speed. But you wouldn't be in class with any of your Malibu friends, and Dad and I wouldn't be able to volunteer in your classroom. If you stay in school here, you'll have to make peace with the bell system, but you'll be in the school you know."

"I want to stay here. I want to go to school with my sister." Justus's voice was worried.

"Then we need to help you learn to live with more structure." I hugged him close. "Do you know who can really turn this situation around for you?"

"My teacher?"

"No, though she can be a big help."

"You and dad? Trinity?"

"Actually, Justus, *you* can make the changes necessary yourself. I know you have it in you to adjust and do fine in school."

In my effort to empower him from the inside out, I had forgotten one Other who could also make a difference. Thankfully, that night at bedtime, when Larry and I both crawled up next to Justus and snuggled close, I thought of another tool we could share with our angry little boy.

"Is this a family meeting?" Justus asked.

45

"No," I laughed. "We're just both very concerned about how unhappy you are at school. And Justus, I have an idea that I think will help you get used to first grade."

"What is it?"

"For lots of years, many Christians have used a special way of praying called the breath prayer to help them through all sorts of times. It's a prayer that you say as you breathe in and out so that the prayer comes naturally." Years of leading spiritual growth retreats for adults had prepared Larry and me to share with our youngest child a helpful and practical spiritual discipline.

Larry added, "Justus, did you know that the Hebrew *ruach* means both 'breath' and 'wind' and 'spirit'? The breath prayer fills you with the spirit of God."

I saw that Justus was focused, taking all this in.

"When you pick a breath prayer," I continued, "you can say it over and over inside yourself. Dad, Trinity, and I can say it with you too, so you'll feel surrounded by our love and God's love as you try to adjust to first grade."

We asked, "What is it you most need from God right now? What is your prayer to God?"

Justus quickly responded, "God, help me feel good at school." That was just right; Justus's behavior could only change if he began to feel good about himself in the school setting.

I had saved the fronts from the previous year's Christmas cards, and Justus chose from the pile of cards a dove picture with the word *PEACE* printed below. On this I carefully printed, God, help me feel good at school. This simple piece of paper became a symbol for Justus of his tangible connection to God.

"When you feel angry, when you feel something welling up inside you, and you know that you're about to do something you'll get in trouble for, take out your card," I told him, "and say your prayer over a few times until you begin to feel calmer." (One of the benefits of the breath prayer is that the repetition of a simple phrase or prayer request actually has a physiological effect; slow, regular breathing does bring about physical peace.)

"Mom and I will repeat your prayer over and over too. So will your sister," Larry said encouragingly. We also called several of the "grandmothers" in our church and even phoned long-distance to Justus's godparents in Chicago, so that they would all support him by praying his breath prayer. We believe, as Paul wrote, that we should "pray all the time, asking for what you need, praying in the Spirit on every possible occasion" (Eph. 6:18, JB).

The next day, Justus took his dove of peace card to school in his backpack. He was on my mind all day as I prayed the prayer he had chosen to meet his current need. Trinity ran up to him on the playground, whispering, "God, help me feel good at school" to let him know she was praying with him too. Justus was surrounded by his personal prayer community.

"How was school today?" I asked that afternoon, trying not to be anxious.

"Better. I only got benched once," he told me, a shy grin spreading over his face. "I had to get my dove card out a few times, but now I think I know my prayer by heart."

The next day, when I picked him up from school, his teacher came up to me. "What has happened to Justus? He is like a different child these last two days." Her voice was low as the children filed past her out the door. "I have *never* seen such dramatic improvement in such a short time. Today, I saw the

Justus you told me was inside that angry little boy. I really like him . . . What has made the difference?"

"Ask *him*," I suggested, smiling, as Justus came to the classroom doorway.

"I like the way you are taking care of yourself, Justus," the teacher said. "What has changed so that you were able to be so helpful?"

Justus reached into his backpack, pulling out the slightly crumpled dove card. "I have a breath prayer. See?" He looked at the card fondly. "And I pray this prayer. So do my mom and dad and sister and some other friends." He grinned. "You know what? God is helping me *really* feel good in first grade. I hardly even notice the bells anymore."

God was a real presence in our son's life. With the psalmist, he could joyfully say, "Blessed are those whose strength is in you" (Psalm 84:5, NIV). Justus not only had a positive first-grade experience; he has continued to use various breath prayers in times of transition, fear, or other need. Just as he has prayers he says with us at meals or bedtime, he also knows that, like David, he can say, "Answer me when I call, O God of my right! You gave me room when I was in distress. Be gracious to me, and hear my prayer" (Psalm 4:1).

The breath prayer card is now in Justus's scrapbook—a reminder of those first difficult weeks of first grade when he felt so angry and alienated. My guess is that in later years, when Justus looks through his scrapbook and sees that blue and white dove, what he will remember most is feeling surrounded by the power of God and the love of God's people. I hope that in learning this age-old spiritual discipline, he will always remember that no matter what the situation, God can be the answer.

Justus has used a breath prayer many times since first grade. A cautious child, he sometimes has difficulty with transitions to new situations. When he is overcome with a lack of confidence, I often say, "Shall we think of a breath prayer that will help you ease your way into this? I can be praying for you today." And my son, fearful and recalcitrant the moment before, usually nods his head emphatically and, quite willingly, trots off to try something new.

Recently, Larry and I were part of the filming of a segment of the television series, "Catch the Spirit." The morning of the filming, as I was getting ready to go, I said to Justus, "I'm feeling nervous about today. I just hope the words come out right, and I say what I mean."

"*You're* nervous?"

"Unfortunately, yes. This is new to me, and I'm not sure what it will be like."

"Do you have a breath prayer?" — question to parent

I stared at my son. "What a good idea!"

"How about, 'Help me not to be scared'?"

"That's good. Maybe even better would be, 'God, help me do my best.' Because if I do my best, I won't need to be scared."

Justus came over to give me a hug. "I'll pray your prayer as much as I can remember to at school today." I felt better knowing my fears were shared by one who knew what it was like to face new situations with uncertainty. When I picked Justus up after the filming, his first words were, "I prayed your breath prayer. How did it go?"

The breath prayer is only one form of prayer that can bring us closer to God. We have tried to encourage Trinity and Justus to maintain an intimate relationship with God through prayer. We started, as most parents do, with nighttime prayer as a way to close each day in God's presence. "God of Day and of Night, of Life and of Death, [we] place [ourselves] into Your holy hands," as Edward Hays has written in his book *Prayers for the Domestic Church* (Forest of Peace Books, Inc., 1979).

Besides other ritualized times of prayer (see *Appreciating God's Good Gifts*, page 33) we model spontaneous prayers that connect us not only to God but to other people. Every time I hear the siren of an ambulance, for instance, I say a brief prayer like "Gracious God, please bless whoever is hurt or sick. Be with them as they are cared for by the paramedics and be with the medical team who tries to help. Send your healing power, O God." Trinity and Justus make up their own prayers in such situations as well.

Our dog, Paws, is a shepherd-husky mix who, whenever he hears the sound of a siren, howls like a wolf, startling the neighborhood as he leans back his head and lets out a mournful wail. When a guest commented on Paws's vocal abilities, Justus replied, "Don't mind him; he's just saying his prayers."

Whenever we see a need that we do not feel able to meet, we ask for God's assistance. For instance, if the kids and I are in a grocery store, and we see a stressed-out mother screaming at her kids, we take a moment to pray for the mother and for the children. If the newspaper headlines are particularly dire, one of us will say a prayer for the starving in Somalia or the victims of violence in Bosnia or the child injured in a gang-related shooting in Los Angeles. These spontaneous prayers are not formal, eyes-closed, and head-bowed activities, but rather are said matter-of-factly with eyes open, as part of the conversation. As we believe God is present in all of life, we assume that God is always listening.

When he was young, a friend of ours named Jason always asked that the connection of hands around a prayer circle not be completed, but that a space be left for Jesus. For our family, God is always the extra unseen presence at our meals, in our travels, wherever we go, and whatever we do.

The Community of Faith

*J*ustus has eclectic musical tastes. For his bedtime listening, he alternates between John Michael Talbot, Ladysmith Black Mambazo, Take Six, Tennessee Ernie Ford, story tapes, and his longtime favorite, James Taylor. One night, when Justus was about four and had been in his bed with the lights out for almost half an hour, I heard him shout, "James Taylor!" I went to his room.

"Do you need something?"

"No, Mom. I was just calling out to James Taylor because he sang, 'If you call out my name, I'll come running!'"

That four-year-old boy took James Taylor's promise seriously that calling for him at any time, any season, would bring him in the name of friendship.

We all need to know that we have friends. God made us for relationship with others, for community.

> *I urge you, then . . . live a life that measures up to the standard God set when [God] called you. Be always humble, gentle, and patient. Show your love by being tolerant with one another. Do your best to preserve the unity which the Spirit gives by means of the peace that binds you together. There is one body and one Spirit, just as there is one hope to which God has called you.*
>
> *—Ephesians 4:1-4,* TEV

It's funny how community can build and flourish for brief intervals in those places where hearts are open with needs shared and expressed. Take the parents' waiting room at a children's hospital. We were there with seven-month-old Justus, hopeful that a simple procedure on his blocked tear ducts would improve his health and eyesight. As we sat in the waiting room, however, we realized that our love for Justus extended to all children.

Ten sets of mothers and fathers, strangers before and after, sat together to share the waiting process while their young ones had minor surgeries for blocked tear ducts, hernias, and ear tubes. We all sat, separate in our own worries, until the first child was brought out. At the squeak of the recovery room door, all eyes glanced over to see a nurse carrying a two-year-old towhead. "Michael's parents?" A woman and man jumped up to enfold little Michael in a family hug. The other parents looked sympathetically at Michael's family, lovingly at their own spouse, and then smiled encouragingly to support the other parents. Here community was formed.

Every time a child was brought from the recovery room and placed in his or her parent's arms, we felt a palpable wave of celebration. Never having met one another before, we loved and enjoyed one another's children. Our hearts caught in our throats when Letty clutched her mother's shirt and wailed, "It hurts, Momma, it hurts!" When Brian refused all liquids we were concerned. We knew he could not be discharged until he'd kept down the required volume of liquid. We laughed when Michelle, as she began to perk up, declared, "Now, where's my wheelchair?" We looked lovingly at Ernie, who almost instantly fell asleep on his father's chest, home at last. We empathized with each young patient who would wake up in the recovery room feeling strange from the effects of the anesthetics and alone among strangers.

We did not talk a lot, other than to exchange important information such as the exact ages of our children. We were not totally present to one another; each family unit primarily focused on itself. But we were present to one another in a subtle way. Perhaps we were a community of care for a specific space and time only, but we also were a reminder of the understanding, compassion, and support that parents everywhere share.

That day of Justus's surgery gave us a glimpse into the community that is possible when people participate in a coming together of hearts. As Christians, we experience numerous instances where community is formed for the long or short term. Our family has found community on a variety of levels: local church congregations, the larger denominational grouping of the United Methodist annual conference, a California-based group of families that has gathered regularly over eight years, and a nongeographic covenant community that has sustained us for more than the sixteen years of our marriage.

Extended contact with others is not the only way Christian community is formed. We have been welcomed and accepted by sisters and brothers in Christ around the world. One Sunday when we were traveling across the country as part of our year-long sabbatical, we dropped by a small United Methodist church in Oklahoma. Larry, Trinity, and I were dressed casually for travel and felt out of place as we walked into a sanctuary filled with people in suits and lovely dresses. Within a few minutes, however, we were no longer conscious of how we looked. We were surrounded by caring, which included an invitation to join the congregation for a potluck after worship. We have found similar welcome in churches in Sierra Leone, England, Ireland, and New Zealand.

In each local parish we have served, we have found love and acceptance in the community of faith. Each congregation has welcomed us from the moment of our arrival, helping us to move in, bringing us meals, and caring for our children.

Each of the five congregations that have been part of our ministry has been unique. We have been blessed by ministry with Hispanics, Native Americans, and a Korean congregation. We have served a white clapboard church on a lake in Michigan, three churches in southeast Los Angeles, and now have spent eight years in a small parish near the Pacific Ocean. In each place we have found kindred spirits with whom we have journeyed for a space of time, united in Jesus Christ.

Paul wrote to the church at Philippi,

> *Your life in Christ makes you strong, and his love comforts you. You have fellowship with the Spirit, and you have kindness and compassion for one another. I urge you, then, to make me completely happy by having the same thoughts, sharing the same love, and being one in soul and mind. . . . be humble toward one another, always considering others better than yourselves. And look out for one another's interests, not just for your own. The attitude you should have is the one Christ Jesus had.*
>
> —Philippians 2:1-5, TEV

I'm not sure I would go so far as to say that we have the same thoughts as all of our parishioners. But I do know that something precious happens when people gather together in the name of Jesus to worship and pray, to serve and reach out to others, and to share their lives. In our Malibu congregation Trinity and Justus have a wide collection of aunts and uncles, grandmas and grandpas, cousins, and friends. Most of their lives have been spent among these people. They are family.

The annual conference (a geographical grouping of churches in United Methodism) provides another network of support for us. Trinity and Justus especially love the annual June meetings where they can reunite with a variety of adult and child friends who come together for a week. Even the place of meeting, the University of Redlands, feels like home to them.

For eight years, we also have met with a smaller representation of the annual conference, a group of four families who provide support and challenge for one another. Because each family is parented by a clergy couple, we share many concerns and needs in terms of family life, career, faith, and values. As all of us are trying to raise our children with an emphasis on peacemaking, inclusiveness, and spirituality, our gatherings include worship and political action as well as sharing what's happening in our lives. The Paloma Community (named for the Spanish word for dove) has been an important friendship network.

Since before we were married, Larry and I have been part of Sisbros, a unique group of friends, which has sustained us through the changes of our lives over the past seventeen years. The following statement from our covenant explains more about who we are as Sisbros:

Sisbros (Sisters and Brothers) is a non-geographic community of faith which was created in 1975 out of a need for supportive connection and a commitment to social and economic justice. We have grown together in a covenant community, sharing specific disciplines which have developed out of our commitment to spirituality, justice, and equality in our lives and throughout the world.

We are a people of biblical faith who believe that a liberating God creates us and enables us to be in covenant community. As people of faith we see in Jesus Christ a paradigm for personal wholeness, faithful relationships, and a new order of justice.

Over the years, we in Sisbros have developed a series of disciplines—"ways we embody and grow in our relationship with one another, our faith, and our world." As a community, we share spiritual disciplines, economic disciplines, and political disciplines, as well as follow specific guidelines for coming together and sharing our lives. Trinity and Justus have known this community all their lives. Every summer and most winters, my children have gathered with a group that loves and affirms them and offers a strong model of living in faith.

In Sisbros, Justus and Trinity see a wide variety of individuals who share commitments and work at relationship together. We come from many parts of the United States; one of our families now lives in Cuba. We span all ages from newborn to retirement. Some of our young adults have grown up in Sisbros and now make their own commitment to the group.

Some of the adults who used to change my children's diapers and rock them to sleep now take them sailing, play swimming games with them, and encourage their volleyball skills. Trinity and Justus have unique relationships with each member of Sisbros, including private jokes and shared history. Sisbros not only provides a model for living for them; it is like an extended family group as well.

Our family is fortunate to have so much support for who we are and who we are trying to become. Not only do we have supportive (biological) family members who nurture us in love, but we also have these communities of faith that call out the best in us. We know that the call to follow Jesus is not easy. We need all the help we can get, so we surround ourselves with people who nurture us in a strong relationship to God and challenge us to faithfulness.

Paul wrote extensively to groups of people who were trying to discern what it means to follow Jesus and to live as his loving community. In these words to the church at Rome, Paul gave practical advice to the community of faith:

> *Love must be completely sincere. Hate what is evil, hold on to what is good. Love one another warmly as Christian brothers [and sisters], and be eager to show respect for one another. Work hard and do not be lazy. Serve the Lord with a heart full of devotion. Let your hope keep you joyful, be patient in your troubles, and pray at all times. Share your belongings with your needy fellow Christians, and open your homes to strangers.*
> —Romans 12:9-13, TEV

Working for Justice

Sing "Let there be light," liltingly and happily. These words became a family code for us when we heard storyteller Michael Parent share an Iroquois tale about animals in the forest who held a council to decide if they should have light in the midst of an all-dark world. This story presented two main characters with opposing opinions.

Bear adamantly growled, "We must have darkness." This ended most discussion since Bear, by virtue of its size and gruffness, carried a lot of weight in the council of animals. Young Chipmunk, however, undaunted by Bear's power, bravely sang out, "Let there be light," again and again until the sun actually spread its gleam throughout the forest world. The story ends with Bear's walking menacingly toward Chipmunk, who runs quickly into a tree for safety but ends up with Bear-clawed stripes on its back as a permanent reminder of the conflict between light and darkness.

In our family, if a conflict is brewing or one person is behaving particularly "Bearlike," someone will sing "Let there be light" as a loving reminder that the darkness can be overcome. (At least one person must feel light-filled, and thus be able to discern the need for early intervention before a storm brews into full force. It also requires that we be able to laugh at ourselves and put our grumpiness into perspective. To have such a perspective is not always easy or possible at a given moment!)

Years ago, I took three children (ages three, six, and nine) to see a "Care Bears" movie. Knowing little about these furry friends, I was surprised to find that the story line contained a strong message: "If we all band together in love, we will be stronger than the world's evil." As in most children's tales, good overcame evil but only after many setbacks and scary moments. At one point, I had all three kids in my lap, clutching me tightly. "I'm scared!" "What's going to happen?" "I hope it turns out all right!"

Knowing the predictability of such movies, I wanted to reassure the children that the Care Bears and crew would indeed save the world from uncaring. On the other hand, I resisted the ease with which Hollywood might present such an ending. I tried to put it in theological terms. "The light is always stronger than the darkness. The darkness never wins in the long run." That made them feel better. When the evil spirit and her magician assistant seemed to gain ground, one of the children would say, "The light's stronger than the darkness. The darkness won't win."

Every time I heard that phrase in the movie, I wondered if, in helping these children deal with the movie's scary parts, I was failing to prepare them for the world in which they live. I could think of countless situations in which the darkness seems alive and well: homeless people on our city streets, war in the Middle East, torture and murder in Central America, starvation in Africa. Does the light really overcome the darkness, or is this phrase a fairy tale in itself?

The question has remained with me. In 1985 I marched in a Pledge of Resistance demonstration in Philadelphia. I wrestled with the question of whether our march through the streets to the

Federal Building would have much impact. Could I make any difference in U.S. foreign policy? *Would* the light indeed overcome the darkness?

In the crannies of my soul, rationality conversed with faith. Was I a naive idealist, surrounded by other dreamers, all misguidedly convinced that we could have an impact on the world? Or was I acting in a faith-filled and realistic way? Was there a guarantee that I would ever see the "peace on earth" for which I so fervently prayed? Yet how would I feel if I gave up prayer because it sometimes seemed a futile pastime?

As a parent, how do I share these struggles with my children? Old conversations, new twists: the issues change in focus even as the basic dilemma presents itself from generation to generation. The particular issue might be U.S. policy toward Central America or disarmament between the superpowers. Who can predict the form that future issues might take? In all such issues, the basic conflict follows the outline of much of the Care Bears movie: good against evil.

As I marched along Chestnut Street, biblical images flooded my mind. "The people who walked in darkness have seen a great light" (Isa. 9:2). "I am the light of the world" (John 8:12). "Now, let us walk as children of light" (Eph. 5:8). I felt a new buoyancy as I reviewed the meaning of light in our faith history. I hummed parts of the *Messiah* in my head.

There has been a stark contrast between the darkness and the light since the Creator first placed light in the sky to overcome the total darkness of the universe. The bottom line for my own involvement has come most specifically through two Scripture passages that have a cause-effect relationship: "The Word was the source of life, and this life brought light to [humankind]. The light shines in the darkness, and the darkness has never put it out" (John 1:4-5, TEV). Because of this, "You yourselves used to be in the darkness, but since you have become the Lord's people, you are in the light. So you must live like people who belong to the light, for it is the light that brings a rich harvest of every kind of goodness, righteousness, and truth" (Eph. 5:8-9, TEV).

Holding my "U.S. OUT OF CENTRAL AMERICA" poster, I came (again) to realize that my participation in such a demonstration was not contingent on the effectiveness of such an action (though I pray and believe such actions can have effect). I was walking to the Federal Building because, as one of "the Lord's people," I believed that light would overcome darkness. I walked to bring the light of "goodness, righteousness, and truth."

I walked not only for myself and my convictions; I walked also as the parent of a three-year-old daughter and an infant son. I walked because I wanted my children to begin to realize that God's power can transform the bleakest situation, even the most evil of deeds. Justus, riding in a backpack, added his own presence in favor of light. Three-year-old Trinity asked questions that forced me to articulate my political views, my spiritual groundings, my hopes and dreams for a new world. As I explained myself in age-appropriate terms, I was reminded again why I march, write letters, and pray in the belief that "the light will overcome the darkness." I shared with each of my children my faith that God is ultimately in charge of the world.

I also shared with them the reality of this world's present darkness in some of the forms it takes. I don't have to detail the gruesomeness of extremist murders in Central America; I may explain that, "There are some people who kill other people." Rather than leaving my children frightened and powerless in the face of such killing, I shared with them the strength that came as we prayed together for the murdered and the murderers in Central America. Then, as now, we acknowledged the darkness; we anticipate the coming of light. Together we can feel the strength of small Chipmunk singing light against growling Bear's "We must have darkness."

Darkness comes in many guises: the violence that tore apart Central America, the evil spirit in the Care Bears movie, bullying Bear's conviction that we must have darkness. To all forms of darkness, we sing liltingly and happily: "Let there be light."

Relying on God's Strength

*L*arry and I try to foster a sense of physical well-being in our children so they can know themselves to be strong of body, mind, and spirit. Larry's family has always been very sports-minded. My growing up did not include any team sports, and I have always regretted that I did not have or take the chance to become skilled at a particular sport. So, since our town has a well-organized system of year-round sports, our children have played on teams since they first expressed an interest in soccer, basketball, or t-ball.

I want my children to trust their bodies and know their physical strength. There is a certain exhilaration in running the length of a soccer field toward the goal or in deftly stealing the basketball from the other team to make two points. It feels good to repeat skills enough in practice that, at game time, one's body knows just what to do and how to do it.

It is also important to learn how to work as a team. The year that Trinity felt tormented by a fifth-grade "group," she also played on a soccer team that included most of the girls in that clique. On the field, distinctions of name-brand clothes and who was "in" disappeared; all the girls worked together, concentrating on the game. Both of our children have found that they can be teammates with people with whom they might not be friends.

Team sports involve developing a common goal (playing well; winning, if possible) that is larger than any of the separate players. All members of the team are important, even if some are more skilled than others. Team sports require the discipline of listening to a coach who keeps the total picture in mind when individual players may see only their own perspective.

Trinity and Justus have each experienced seasons of being the undefeated champs, of not winning a single game, and of winning some and losing some. Both winning and losing teach important lessons, and a season of never winning is not necessarily a "bad" season.

When Justus first played soccer at age five, he instinctively seemed to know which way to run and what to do with the ball. He has been an "all-star" every year that he's played. However, we were reminded recently that physical strength is only one aspect of success in sports.

Justus had a hard time making up his mind to play soccer this year. When one of our children makes a decision (such as "I don't want to play soccer,") that usually concludes the subject. But, for some reason, I wouldn't let go of the fact that Justus loves to play, is very good at soccer, and might feel left out once soccer season came and he saw his sister and friends playing without him.

My decision to continue offering him the opportunity to change his mind was not, I now realize, a smart move. Knowing that Justus tends to be hesitant at some points, I encouraged him to play. I thought I knew what was best for him instead of letting his "no" be "no." In hindsight (too late now), I should have accepted his first answer and let him sit out a season.

With my prodding, Justus finally decided to play, but I'm not sure his heart was in it as before. He pulled ligaments in the first game and had to sit out the next two. The third game, Justus played goalie and made some incredible saves, earning the respect of teammates and parents.

"You were wonderful out there!" I said as I hugged him after the game.

"I hate it. It's scary playing goalie."

"I can believe that. It looked like you had six pairs of feet in your face at one point."

Justus's team had two good practices that next week. When I picked him up after one practice, his coach was giving a pep talk about what it means to be a team.

"I need each of you to play your hardest. You don't have to be a star; you don't have to be the best on the team. I just want you to play hard and do your best," the coach explained. "When it's time for me to pick the all-stars, I will look not only for who played well but for who was cooperative, who pulled for the team and encouraged other players, and who played hard regardless of skill level.

"I'm the coach. I make the decisions about who plays where, and my decisions are final. I can't listen to every one of you telling me where you want to play because that would be chaos. So please listen to what I decide and play your best wherever I put you."

On the way home, Justus and I talked about the coach's words.

"I'm ready to play hard and listen to the coach," Justus said.

On game day, Trinity and I dropped Justus off at the field, then quickly ran a couple of errands before his game started. When we returned to the field, the game had begun. Justus sat on the sidelines, looking mournful.

"I couldn't play without you here," he said sadly.

"I'm sorry we're late, but I don't accept responsibility for your not playing," I replied. "You knew we'd be here and now we are, ready to watch you play."

"The coach said I had to play goalie." Something in my son's tone of voice made me listen carefully.

"I'm really scared to play goalie."

"It makes sense to be scared. It's a hard position. But you are very good at it, and the coach seems to think that you are the best one to play that position today."

"But I *hate* goalie!"

"Remember what the coach said yesterday about listening to him and playing where he put you?"

"But I'm scared!"

I paused, trying to decide how to proceed. Justus has had other times of fearfulness when a little encouragement helped him get past the fear.

"Are you going to let the fear be the strongest part of you? Don't you think that somewhere inside of you is enough courage to face the fear?"

"No!"

I tried a different tactic. "Your team needs you. You don't want to let the team down, do you?"

"I'm scared!" His eyes were wide, and he sat with his arms wrapped around himself as if cold.

"Why don't we come up with a breath prayer for you? I can sit and pray for you while you play." No response.

The referee called the quarter, and the coach came over to where we sat.

"Ready to play goalie, Justus?"

"No. I hate it!"

"Then I guess you'll sit this quarter out too."

I stared down at the grass underneath me. I felt caught between a rock and a hard place. On the one hand, I wanted Justus to get past his fear. On the other hand, if this was a day he felt fearful, maybe goalie was just too much to handle. I understood the coach's wanting to pull authority and be "the coach." And Justus was the best goalie on the team (which was now behind in points).

Yet here was a child who wanted to play, was dressed out in his uniform and willing to play any position on the field except goalie, and he sat on the side because of a battle of stubborn wills.

When it was halftime, the coach came again to Justus.

"Ready to play goalie?"

"No."

The coach walked off. Suddenly, Justus was surrounded by his teammates.

"Please play goalie, Justus."

"We need you, Justus."

"Just one quarter, Justus, please! We're behind. We need you."

Justus sat, shaking his head, while the other boys moved away from him in disappointment. He looked in anguish at me. "I'm just a 'fraidy cat.' "

I found the pressure hard to take. His decision was not my decision, yet I felt judged by the other kids, their parents, and the coach. I'm sure these feelings came from inside of me, not from them. I found myself speaking the dreaded words to my son out of my own inner pressures rather than in response to what he was doing.

"Justus, I'm disappointed in you. I'm disappointed that you won't at least give it a try. One quarter is all you need to play.

Your team needs you. How are you going to feel if your team loses? You're letting down your team. I know you're scared, but I still wish you'd try."

Even as I said this, it felt like a script from some old movie. Justus didn't need me to get down on him. My job as a parent was to be his cheerleader and advocate, not to take the side of others against him. Yet how did that tie in with teaching responsibility and teamwork and facing fears?

I got up to walk along the sidelines, needing a break. The coach came over to me.

"I hope you understand that I need to make a point with Justus. If I let him get away with not being goalie, then all the boys will think they can be in charge of the team. Next game, he can play any position he wants."

"He's a fearful child, and today is a hard day for him," I tried to explain. The whole world of sports felt very foreign to me right now. I didn't belong here. I walked back to our chair.

Seeing Justus sit, defeated, watching his team get further and further behind, I moved closer and put my arm around him. He was only eight years old. Soccer was just a game. His well-being was far more important than whether the team won or lost that day. By the time the coach came by at the end of the third quarter ("Ready to play goalie?"), I had softened toward my son, though occasionally a preachy and unhelpful repetition of something I'd said earlier would come out of my mouth.

The game ended. Justus's team lost. We left the field, and I apologized to my son, the erstwhile goalie.

"You know, Justus, sometimes I have a hard time understanding you. Trinity and I are a lot alike, and even she surprises me sometimes. But you and I are different in so many ways, I don't know how to help you. I'm sorry if I didn't give you enough support just now." We walked along, holding hands. "I don't really know how it feels to have your fear of being goalie. I only see how well you've played the position. I love you, and I'll try to give you more support."

Justus didn't respond. He'd had enough of grownups talking at him. And I knew that, as much as I understood the coach, Larry and I would need to share with him our feelings about what had happened at this game.

I realized again that physical strength is nothing if not propelled from the inside by a strong sense of self. None of us can succeed on the outside if we do not feel undergirded on the inside.

Paul wrote to the church at Ephesus about what it means to be strong:

> *Finally, build up your strength in union with the Lord and by means of [God's] mighty power. Put on all the armor that God gives you, . . . So stand ready, with truth as a belt tight around your waist, with righteousness as your breastplate, and as your shoes the readiness to announce the Good News of peace. At all times carry faith as a shield. . . . And accept salvation as a helmet, and the word of God as the sword which the Spirit gives you. Do all this in prayer, asking for God's help.*
>
> —Ephesians 6:10-11a, 14-18, TEV

It would take God and all of us to help Justus build up his strength "by means of God's mighty power." As good as it is that he can run fast and kick well and hit a baseball far into the field, isn't it more important that he understand himself to be loved by God? Isn't it more important that he know who he is as a child of God and act accordingly?

On the way home from the game I said, trying to be encouraging, "Justus, don't call yourself a 'fraidy cat.' Little by little, you are growing out of this fearful stage. I can think of a lot of situations you face bravely now that used to scare you. You're improving."

"*Slowly* improving," he said, so seriously that I had to laugh and hug him close.

"Moving at your own pace," I said, determined that he judge himself by an inner yardstick; not by the judgments of coach, teammates, or others.

Larry and I as parents know that inner strength and emotional security are more important than outward courage. It is our job to help both of our children move toward the point where they can handle new situations in confidence without us. How do we prepare our children for what lies ahead? We start by walking with them through what we now see (soccer games, violin recitals, the death of a pet, problems with math) and undergird them, not only with our own unswerving love, but with the love of God who can be there even when we are not.

We can help them to have a greater goal than what may be obviously at hand—the goal of being true to their calling as Christians.

> *All this I do for the gospel's sake, in order to share in its blessings. Surely you know that many runners take part in a race, but only one of them wins the prize. Run,*

then, in such a way as to win the prize. Every athlete in training submits to strict discipline, in order to be crowned with a wreath that will not last; but we do it for one that will last forever. That is why I run straight for the finish line.

—1 Corinthians 9:23-26, TEV

I hope that Trinity and Justus will continue to enjoy the strength of their bodies in sports and an active life. More important, however, I pray that they will understand that relationship to God means relying on God's strength even when they feel unequal to a task. "I have the strength to face all conditions by the power that Christ gives me" (Phil. 4:13, TEV).

Making Choices

I guess there must be some new fad at school," Trinity said matter-of-factly at the beginning of fifth grade. "I'm finding out there's a right and wrong style of clothing to wear."

"What is the popular way?" I asked.

"I don't know," Trinity replied. "But whatever it is, I sure don't have it. No matter what I wear, 'the group' comes up to tell me how stupid I look. 'What dumb shoes!' they say. Or, 'Where'd you buy those pants?' in a voice that's no compliment."

My heart crumbled into little pieces. "That must make you feel terrible."

"Not really. I'm used to it. If you're not in 'the group,' it's hard to do anything right *in their eyes.*"

I put down the mixer, setting aside the cookies I was making to sit down at the counter with my daughter and hear what was happening to her.

She told me who was in the group—almost all girls she had known since preschool—nice girls until they began to exclude most of the rest of the fifth-grade class as "unacceptable." As Trinity told me things these girls were doing or saying to her and others, I felt a tremendous sadness for all of the children involved.

"So do you ever think about changing schools?"

Her words stopped me cold: "I think about it every day."

The mother-protector in me flew into action. "Well, we could at least look into the Catholic school. Maybe things would be easier for you there."

"Mom," my nine-year-old said patiently, "there will be kids like this at every school."

That made sense, but I pressed on. "At the Catholic school, at least you'd be wearing a uniform so they couldn't bug you about your clothes."

"They would find something to tease me about. Kids like that are good at finding ways to make other kids feel miserable." Trinity looked evenly at me. "Mom, I just have to learn to deal with it."

Fifth grade brought some difficult moments for Larry and me as we heard of 'the group's' various methods of torture. Another parent called to see if I wanted to join her in going to the principal about the problem. The group was following other kids around, taunting them about clothes, possessions, and anything else they could think of. I asked Trinity if she thought it would help for me and her friend's mother to go to the principal.

"I don't need you to do that, Mom. I'm handling it." Trinity looked at me mischievously. "I don't say mean things back to them. But I do call them 'the Klan' instead of 'the group' even though I don't think they get what I mean." I found it interesting that my daughter made the connection between a bunch of fifth graders wanting control of the playground and the Ku Klux Klan's desire for power.

One day, Trinity came home and said nonchalantly, "The group asked me to join them today."

"And you said . . . ?"

"I told them that even though I like most of them by themselves, I don't like the way they treat other people when they are a group. So I said No."

This child was teaching me a lot about standing up for one's beliefs. Throughout the school year, as 'the group' continued to exclude Trinity and many others, I was amazed at how matter-of-factly she dealt with what seemed to be painful situations.

"I really admire how you're handling all of this, Trinity."

"Oh, it's just part of life."

I thought back to Trinity's kindergarten year when we had our first crisis of trust in our older child. At that time, she would have followed any group anywhere. Now she had a strong sense of who she was and who she wanted to be.

When she started kindergarten, Trinity began to bring home small toys that she said other children had given her or she'd won as a prize. We found some of these stories hard to believe, but our daughter had always been honest and trustworthy.

One day at sharing time, Trinity pulled a puppet called "Miss Muffy" out of her backpack. The problem was that this puppet belonged not to Trinity but to the teacher, who promptly talked to her about not taking things that were not hers. The next day, Trinity and two friends took some stickers from the teacher's desk. The other children hid their stickers but, new to the game, Trinity was caught because she showed her stickers to everyone in the class.

Larry and I were floored when the kindergarten teacher, a friend of ours, came to talk to us about our daughter's behavior. It seemed that Trinity was trying hard to fit in with some of the other children and was going along with their plan of action without thinking through her own appropriate response.

"I didn't do it!" she pouted. "I don't care what the teacher said." Since we hadn't mentioned any details of what the teacher told us, Trinity's guilt was clear. Knowing that barely-five-year-old children are still developing a consciousness of right and wrong, we were careful not to attach words like *stealing* and *lying* to this behavior and decided to concentrate on the issue of honesty.

"I think we need to talk," I said to Trinity, who clammed up tight and refused to discuss any but the most mundane matters at home.

"I'm not talking about it!" she insisted, even though we hadn't said what we needed to talk about.

Finally, one day as we were driving home from school, I said, "Trinity, I feel hurt when you put up a wall and shut me out." I struggled to find words that expressed my feelings in a way she would understand. "To me, love is sharing, listening, working things through. I need to know how you're feeling."

My words were met with silence. Once we were home, however, Trinity came to sit on my lap in our special chair. She talked about how angry she was at her teacher for bringing her parents in on this and about how the kids who got into trouble seemed to get the most attention. She had known it was wrong to take things from the teacher's desk, but she wanted to be part of a group.

"Trinity, I know you are strong enough to say no to your friends when they suggest actions you think are wrong. In the long run, you'll see that you get positive attention from your teacher if you do your best work and follow the rules."

As we sat and rocked, Trinity's brusque exterior of the past days mellowed.

"Are you mad at me?" she asked, face serious.

"No, we're not mad at you. It may just be hard to trust you right away. That's why we need to have absolute honesty in our family. I'd much rather you tell me the truth, even if it isn't what I want to hear, than lie to me.

"You know how when your teacher cleans off the chalkboard, where there used to be words, then it's all clean?" I asked her. I could tell she was paying attention. "Well, that's how it is with forgiveness. Anything we do wrong is like those words on the chalkboard. When God forgives us, the board is wiped clean."

I hugged her close. "Now that we've worked this out, let's consider this a new beginning. From now on, I know you'll be ready to do the right thing and always tell the truth."

This family policy has continued: tell the truth, no matter what. The policy holds true for all of us, even though there are times when we have to be honest about things we'd rather hide. "I want to know that I can trust you completely," I've told my children, "so that if an adult ever says something about you that isn't true, I'll be able to believe you and stick up for you."

This has proved necessary at times when an adult who didn't know my children jumped to an inappropriate conclusion and blamed them for something they did not do. One teacher, for instance, accused Trinity of stealing a pair of scissors from her class, even though we had purchased scissors for Trinity and had even written her name on them. The teacher took away the scissors, leaving Trinity feeling shamed and humiliated.

When I went in to talk to the teacher about this, she asked, "Can you prove that these scissors were hers?" Since these were the inexpensive, generic silver scissors of countless classrooms, I responded, "No, I can't prove that these exact scissors are hers, but I do know that I purchased a pair just like this for her to have at her desk. And I also know that my child doesn't lie."

The teacher, who made an entire year miserable for us, looked at me disdainfully. "All parents think their children don't lie."

"That may be the case but I stand behind Trinity. You can keep these scissors. I'll buy her another pair."

I knew I could believe my child, so I stood up for her in the face of an insensitive and uncaring adult. I know that my kids are there for me as well. I try to be honest with both children about who I am, even though this may include sharing about times when I am less than exemplary.

Both children have participated in D.A.R.E., a drug and alcohol education program. We have had numerous discussions about the effects of substance addiction on individuals and society. Trinity and Justus know that Larry and I choose not to drink out of solidarity with the many people whose lives have been torn apart by alcohol or drug abuse. Yet, when asked "Did you ever drink, Mom?" I chose to be honest.

"There was a three- or four-year period in my life when I thought it was fun to occasionally go out to a bar with friends," I admitted. "It was at the end of college and drinking made me feel grown up." I looked at my two most precious gifts from God. "It wasn't a terrible time in my life, but it's not something I'm proud of."

"Did you ever get drunk?" Justus asked.

"Not really. I was careful not to drink too much, but I can still remember wondering if others could tell that I was having to concentrate hard on what I was saying and doing." I paused, remembering the gaiety of young adults gathered around a table in a bar, casually sipping wine or fancy drinks. "Even when I drank only a small amount, I could feel the effects. My coordination was off-balance just enough that I couldn't trust myself. It wasn't a fun feeling, being slightly out of control."

"Were you ever drunk like people in the movies?" Trinity wondered.

"No, but I'm sure there were times when I drank more than I should have. I don't feel good about those times. I'm sure I could have had just as much fun without the alcohol. I just thought being grown up meant drinking. Since neither of my parents ever drank, it was a way of rebelling. Pretty silly, huh?"

"Yeah, Mom," Justus replied. "Too bad you didn't have D.A.R.E. like we do."

"You're right. If I'd learned all you're learning about drugs and alcohol, I would have known better than to follow the crowd and try to prove myself." Once again, a discussion with my children helped me to put my own life in perspective. Thanks to the constant love of my family and God, I didn't get more involved in addictive behaviors.

My parents' love always undergirded me, subtly reminding me to be the best I could. There were no threats of "If you ever . . . we'll throw you out of the house." High expectations and constant affirmation called me to remember who and Whose I was. These words of Paul to the church at Philippi illustrate the way my own parents nurtured me to follow God's path rather than that of the 'in group':

> *So then, dear friends, as you always obeyed me when I was with you, it is even more important that you obey me now while I am away from you. Keep on working with fear and trembling to complete your salvation,*

because God is always at work in you to make you willing and able to obey [God's] own purpose.

Do everything without complaining or arguing, so that you may be innocent and pure as God's perfect children, who live in a world of corrupt and sinful people. You must shine among them like stars lighting up the sky, as you offer them the message of life. If you do so, I shall have reason to be proud of you on the Day of Christ, because it will show that all my effort and work have not been wasted.

—Philippians 2:12-16, TEV

Trinity and Justus must find their own ways in the world. Our task as parents includes love and affirmation, modeling, and faith-sharing. As all people, our children will be tested numerous times as they grow and develop their own standards for living. If they understand that God is always at work in them, they will be able to make choices that are healthy for mind, body, and spirit. As a parent, I need to trust their decisions, even though those decisions may be different from those I would make for them.

Paul lifts up some important standards for living and decision-making in his letter to the Philippians: "Finally, beloved, whatever is true, whatever is honorable, whatever is just, whatever is pure, whatever is pleasing, whatever is commendable, if there is any excellence and if there is anything worthy of praise, think about these things" (Phil. 4:8, NRSV). My prayer is that whatever pressures come their ways, Trinity and Justus will be strong enough to remain true to themselves and to their faith, facing life with honesty, a positive attitude, and an inner strength which does not need to follow the crowd.

Living as God's People

Read matt. 5:13 - 16

Justus and I were chatting away as we pulled up to the stoplight.

When we saw the grizzled-looking man on the corner, holding his "Will Work for Food" sign, however, we fell silent.

Justus's voice was quiet. "Do you think anyone will hire him today?"

"I don't know. I know he needs work, but I don't know how many people would feel comfortable hiring someone off the streets to work in their homes." I looked over at the man, noticing his ragged clothes and shopping bag. I sighed. "But it breaks my heart to see him there."

"It breaks my heart too," Justus admitted.

The light changed, and we continued on our way.

"I want to help everybody," I told my young son, "but sometimes it's hard to know the best way to help."

We drove along Pacific Coast Highway, admiring the sunlight glinting off the ocean waves, both of us lost in our thoughts.

"Mom," Justus said, calling me from my reverie. "I'm glad there are ways we *do* help. Sometimes we take care of people's kids when they're having a rough time."

I thought of two families whose children we have tried to incorporate into our family to give support to the parents, who need to attend twelve-step meetings in order to stay clean and sober.

"And you and Dad do a lot of talking with people who have problems. Also we give money to groups that work with homeless people." Justus sounded more cheerful now.

"Right," I responded. "And the 'Bible Kids' do a lot—cleaning up trash, visiting older adults who may be lonely, making lunches for homeless people in Malibu."

"We can't do everything, but I'm glad we can do *something*," Justus concluded.

That conversation has stayed in my mind, just as the face of that man on the street corner occasionally haunts me. The world has so much pain. I want my children to be cognizant of the needs of God's children everywhere, but I do not want them to be overwhelmed into passive withdrawal.

> *My brothers [and sisters], what good is it for someone to say that [they have] faith if [their] actions do not prove it? Can that faith save [them]? Suppose there are brothers or sisters who need clothes and don't have enough to eat. What good is there in your saying to them, "God bless you! Keep warm and eat well!"—if you don't give them the necessities of life? So it is with faith: if it is alone and includes no actions, then it is dead.*
>
> —James 2:14-17, TEV

Trinity and Justus need to feel connected to the anguish of the world's need. They also need to know that their efforts do make a difference. As a family, we seek to act out our faith in a variety of ways.

Because we take Jesus' statement seriously, "Blessed are the peacemakers" (Matt. 5:9), we have often included our children in protests and demonstrations for peace. It is not always easy to explain a complex political situation in simple terms, but once we try, I am amazed at how my children grasp the situation and crystalize their own meaning from it. Trinity and Justus are there because it makes sense to them, not just because it is important to their parents.

When we have gone to the Nevada Test Site outside of Las Vegas, joining with other families in the Paloma Community, the children have made origami paper cranes (modeled after the story *Sadako and the Thousand Paper Cranes*). One year, the Paloma children took a collection of colorful cranes over to the men who guarded the crossing gate into the test site.

"Here," the children said, offering a string of cranes to the uniformed men. "Pray for peace." The officers, whose job was to keep peace protesters out of the test site, cheerfully thanked the children and accepted their gift. It was a wonderfully humanizing moment, reminding all of us that no matter which side of the line we stood on, we were connected.

I want my children to make careful choices about how they live out their faith. I also want them to respect other people's choices which may differ from their own. Part of living as God's people is being open to the understandings and perspectives of others.

One day as we were driving along, Trinity gave me some new ideas. Out of the blue she said, "I don't think people would listen to Jesus if he came today."

Read page 88 & 89

I was instantly attentive. Trinity is not usually one to bring up theological discussions.

"Oh? Why not?"

"Everyone's too busy. I can't imagine people standing around on a hillside to hear what he was saying." She paused. "And you can't hear from a limousine."

By this time, I had grabbed a notebook and pen, attempting to jot down her words and drive at the same time. "What about in an auditorium?

"There isn't an auditorium large enough."

"What would Jesus talk about?"

Trinity considered. "Probably about the environment, but there are already other people doing that. You know, when Jesus was alive and preaching, no one threw vegetables at him while he was talking, like they do some speakers now. Then, they knew a savior was coming. They were ready to listen."

Justus, listening from the back seat, asked, "Who would kill him now?"

"Oh, they wouldn't kill him right away." How did she come to be so authoritative? "People now expect Jesus to come, but at the same time, they don't really want him to come. They're afraid of what he'll say or what he'll look like. What if he looks like a snake?" She sighed. "I think it would be hard for Jesus to come to earth now."

"Why?"

"There are too many kinds of people. How could they know who he was? How would he dress so everyone could relate to him?"

I asked another question. "Is there any place Jesus is most likely to return to?"

"Probably Egypt, because they wear turbans. Or Rome or Judea because those are places Jesus knew."

"What places most need Jesus?"

"Los Angeles, Costa Rica, Nicaragua, the world . . . "

We seemed to be on a roll so I asked, "And who would be his disciples?"

"Well," Trinity replied, sounding as if she had carefully thought all this out. "Tons of people would want to be his disciples, but it would be hard to be a really good disciple."

So far, this conversation was like a minicourse in continuing education. "What makes a good disciple?"

"You tell all about Jesus. All ministers would be good disciples, but most people would need instructions to be disciples."

"How would Jesus talk today?"

"He wouldn't use slang. He would talk so people could understand him.

"Actually," Trinity said, as if she'd had a tremendous insight, "I think Jesus would teach us to make huge paper airplanes with peace words on them, so people all over the world would know about peace."

As we arrived at our destination, this illuminating conversation had to come to an end. I thought of those giant paper airplanes floating around the world, and of how hard it is to be a disciple.

> But the wisdom from above is pure first of all; it is also peaceful, gentle, and friendly; it is full of compassion and produces a harvest of good deeds; it is free from prejudice and hypocrisy. And goodness is the harvest that is produced from the seeds the peacemakers plant in peace.
>
> —James 3:17-18, TEV

Peacemaking is more than thinking about wars between nations. It is a way of life that includes all people as brothers and sisters. For our family, peacemaking begins at home—in the way we treat each other, how we work out our differences, who we welcome into our living space.

Our home is a place of hospitality for people from around the world. For fifteen years we have belonged to two host-traveler organizations that promote world peace through sharing one another's homes. Servas International was started after World War II as a way to build bridges between people from different nations. As hosts, we receive travelers from anywhere in the world, offering two or more days free hospitality. Mennonite Your Way is a program of the historic peace churches that offers low-cost visits in private homes.

Since we have traveled extensively with these organizations, we enjoy opening our home and taking foreign visitors into our family for a brief time. Some travelers have become part of our extended family. Brendon and Anne, for instance, first came to us from New Zealand in 1982. We so enjoyed their first visit that they came back several months later after completing their U.S. travels. We corresponded with them for years, and when the four of us went to Wellington in 1990, Brendon and Anne played host to us and gave us the royal treatment! They have been back to see us, and we continue to write letters, eagerly anticipating our next reunion.

I met Kenji and Genevieve while traveling with Servas in 1975. We have remained long-distance friends, celebrating marriages and children's births across the miles. Kenji is a Japanese Buddhist; Genevieve a French Catholic. We have much to learn from one another.

Trinity and Justus have benefited from our international guests. Danish visitor, Morton, helped Larry build a bunk bed for Trinity. Swedish writer, Per, spent Thanksgiving with us one year and helped us appreciate our nation's customs in a new way. German friend, Stephen, played a violin duet with Trinity. Anya and Victor brought gifts to each child from the Soviet Union; Noboyuki shared treats from Japan. These travelers arrive as strangers at our door but are welcomed into our home as friends. Both children enjoy finding out about other countries and customs. They have learned to speak slowly and distinctly so that non-English speakers can understand the conversation and have added words from other languages to their vocabulary as well.

Our children have learned world geography because of our international guests. On a hallway wall in our home, we keep a large world map mounted on a bulletin board. We use stick pins to denote the locations of our friends around the world. From the tiny dot at Wellington, New Zealand, for instance, a string leads out to a picture of Anne and Brendon. Scattered across the board are pictures of many of God's people who reside around the globe. Opening our home to international visitors means opening our hearts to those with experiences quite different from our own.

I want my children to grow up with as few stereotypes and misconceptions about people different than themselves as possible. When I first started working with HIV-positive persons as part of an annual "Strength for the Journey" retreat, I invited some of the participants to visit our home. Before they came, I worked with Trinity and Justus so they would understand the virus, how it is spread, and why these young men especially needed our love.

One young man, Evan, was especially needy. He had run away from his own dysfunctional family at an early age and still did not feel valued by his parents. Evan came frequently to visit and even moved to the Los Angeles area so he could see us more often.

"If I could have had a son," Evan told me, "he would have been just like Justus."

One evening, Evan was walking around the house with Justus, then four, balanced on his shoulders. Surveying the world from well above six feet, Justus said, "Evan, I can hardly wait until I am big enough to give you a ride on my shoulders."

Evan's face was pained as he realized that he would be lucky to make it to his thirtieth birthday, let alone to an age at which Justus would be big enough to carry someone on *his* shoulders.

"Well, sweetheart," I said to my son, trying to ease Evan's pain, "for now, just enjoy taking a ride on Evan's shoulders."

After he had gone home that night, Evan called. "I'm not going to come visit anymore," he said. "It just isn't fair to Justus. I don't want him to have to go through my dying."

"Evan," I responded, "Justus came into this relationship with his eyes wide open. He knows you have AIDS. He doesn't need to worry about the future; he loves you *now*. No matter what happens to you, he will always remember you and what you've meant to him." Evan continued to visit us.

Another time, Evan and Trinity were discussing the fact that she would soon be getting braces on her teeth.

"I have to have braces," Trinity explained, "because when I was younger I sucked my teeth. Braces are my consequence, just like AIDS is your consequence for taking drugs."

Evan was stunned and later told me, "That's the most matter-of-fact acceptance of my disease that I have received from anyone. I'm used to people condemning me for the virus; Trinity compared it to getting braces."

Perhaps the guiding principle for any who wish to live as God's people is the simple phrase from 1 John 4:8: "God is love." Love may mean acceptance of an HIV-positive young man, giving up one's bedroom for a foreign visitor, or handing peace cranes to officers at the Nevada Test Site. Love involves looking at the world's needs and figuring out what I (in my age, stage, and situation) can do to make a difference.

> *You are the people of God; [God] loved you and chose you for [God's] own. So then, you must clothe yourselves with compassion, kindness, humility, gentleness, and patience. Be tolerant with one another and forgive one another whenever any of you has a complaint against someone else. You must forgive one another just as the Lord has forgiven you. And to all these qualities add love, which binds all things together in perfect unity. The peace that Christ gives is to guide you in the decisions you make; for it is to this peace that God has called you together in the one body.*
> —Colossians 3:12-15, TEV

Symbols of Forgiveness

*I*f a person does something wrong, how do they go about making a sacrifice to God?" Justus asked his dad on the way home from school one day.

Larry was slightly taken aback by the question, but answered, "When someone does something wrong, they can talk to God about it and ask for forgiveness."

"But what about making an animal sacrifice at the altar?" It was obvious that this six-year-old had been studying Old Testament practices in Sunday school.

"In the Bible, we read about people making sacrifices like that," Larry tried to explain. "But as Christians, we believe that if we make mistakes, we can go to God and ask for forgiveness."

"Even if it is something terrible?"

Wondering what this was leading up to, Larry responded, "Yes, even if you do something very wrong, you can go to God for forgiveness. And if what you did involved another person, you might ask them to forgive you, as well."

Justus was silent a minute, then turned to his nine-year-old sister, who was reading in the back seat.

"Trinity, I flushed your favorite bracelet down the toilet. Will you forgive me?"

When general theology meets everyday life, everyone comes out a learner. Trinity was incredulous that her brother, in a fit of temper, had taken her favorite bracelet and maliciously flushed it down the toilet. This was unlike anything Justus had ever done.

Hard as it was for the little brother to ask for forgiveness, it was just as hard for the older sister to grant it. We tried to affirm the fact that Justus had chosen to tell his misdeed; without his confession, Trinity might have assumed that she had somehow lost her bracelet. But the fact remained that Justus had destroyed something he knew was precious to his sister.

Many of our family's house rules applied to this messy situation: be considerate of others, state your feelings rather than act out in anger, respect others' property, be honest and forthright. But another of our guidelines also entered the picture: People are always more important than things. In other words, when someone accidentally breaks something (even if it is the family Wedgewood), that person's feelings count more than the value of the possession.

Justus was penitent—even miserable—as he tried to own his negative action; he wanted to receive Trinity's blessing. Trinity, on the other hand, felt that this was almost too much to take.

Though Trinity would forgive Justus she didn't trust him much at this point. By bedtime, the two of them cuddled close together for a chapter or two of a family read-out-loud book. Still, I knew that Trinity had an inner "keep out of my room" sign as far as her brother was concerned.

After the children had gone to bed that night, I reflected on this opportunity to know God's grace in a new way. Jesus had told Peter to forgive wholeheartedly, as many as "seventy times seven" (Matt. 18:22) if necessary. As Paul says, "As the Lord has forgiven you, so you also must forgive" (Col. 3:13).

I knew that Trinity did not hold grudges. But I had also heard Justus ask about "sacrifice." Don't most of us crave a symbol of forgiveness? Maybe we don't require a perfect ram as altar fuel, but what about Paul's charge to the Romans: "Present your bodies as a living sacrifice, holy and acceptable to God"?

In Justus's mind, what he had done was the worst possible thing. "I wish I hadn't done it. I wish I could bring the bracelet back," he moaned.

The bracelet had been special because it was one-of-a-kind, made for Trinity by a friend who had painstakingly taken tiny safety pins, beads, and elastic to create a beautiful piece of art. Though the bracelet was irreplaceable in one sense, the things it was made of were common and quite easy to replace. An idea came to me for a way to help Justus feel that he had made atonement ("sacrifice," in his mind) and to bring the children close again.

When I proposed my idea at the breakfast table the next morning, both children were enthusiastic. Justus would use his own money to buy the supplies. Then the two kids would work together to fashion a new bracelet, symbolizing mutual relationship of forgiver and forgiven. As they grow to adulthood, Trinity and Justus will have many times when one will need to ask for forgiveness from the other. This bracelet would be a reminder of the fact that all of us have times we need to ask for forgiveness and times we need to forgive.

Trinity and Justus enjoyed making the bracelet together. By the time we were finished, we all appreciated the time Trinity's friend had put into the first bracelet. And, as an added benefit, there were enough supplies to make a second bracelet for Justus as well.

"Present your bodies as a living sacrifice." What about those times in our lives when we need to ask forgiveness—of a spouse, a child, a coworker, a friend? What might be tangible symbols of both our authentic penitence and their forgiveness? It might be a greeting card, a bouquet of flowers, an inner recommitment to the relationship. It might be a three-inch by five-inch card on the bathroom mirror on which is written: "Jesus says: 70 X 7."

Each of us needs symbols to remind us that because Jesus Christ died for our sins, we live today in new relationship to God and to each other. The cross, crown of thorns, fish, and other Christian symbols bring home this reality every time we look at them. A colorful bracelet of safety pins and beads reminds at least two children I know that no matter what they do, God is Love, always ready to forgive them.

Sometimes it is easier to accept God's forgiveness for what *we* have done than to forgive someone else for his or her actions. I recently found a card I had made out of red pencil and paper. The handwriting looked to be that of a child eight or nine years old. It was addressed to my father. Whatever the occasion for which I had fashioned the card, it contained a message of love that must have warmed his heart: *"Your* (sic) *great, terrific, neat, cool, fabulas,* (sic) *loving, nice, caring, kind, magnifico. I love you Dad."* When my father reached the end of the card, however, he may not have felt so affirmed. I had signed it *"from Wanda, Anne, Bill. P.S. And 2 dead dogs."*

Only a member of our family could have understood the depth of sentiment in those final four words. It wasn't until my mother was dying that I made an effort to see my parents' side of what I considered to be a betrayal and cruel treatment in the midst of an otherwise bright and sunny childhood.

I had come home from school to find that our two family dogs, Scamper and Mikey, had been taken to the animal shelter. This was not only a surprise—in my mind, it was treachery. I dearly loved those dogs and could not understand why they were no longer to be in our family. I knew that Mikey was seventeen years old, blind and deaf, but I couldn't understand why she should be put to sleep. I understood that my Beagle, Scamper, had been a nuisance most of his life—jumping out of the yard and running around the neighborhood—but in my young eyes, those were not crimes that warranted the animal shelter.

I don't remember my parents including me in making the decision about what to do with these pets. I only remember that when my mother tried to explain where Scamper and Mikey were, I was hurt and furious. For years, when we would see a Beagle from a distance, I wondered out loud if that might be Scamper. The thought that he might have been put to sleep was too much for me to bear.

My parents probably tried to help me with my anger as much as possible; but I remained quietly full of wrath and distrust. My guess is that every once in a while, as in the card to my father, I let loose some equivalent of "and two dead dogs," just to let my parents know that they were not forgiven.

It is only since I myself have become a parent (with a family dog who, though much loved by all of us, was anything but the docile, obedient pet of our dreams), that I have begun to understand some of the feelings my parents must have had. With some trepidation, I brought the subject up to my mother. I wanted to be gentle and understanding, but had built up almost thirty years of resentment. She told me that neighbors had complained, and that Scamper had been in trouble with the electric company for his digging. My parents' decision made more sense to me now that I too was a parent with a troublesome dog.

I knew it was time to forgive my mother and father. I don't think they were aware of the little-girl hurt still deep inside me, and I wished they had included me in that fateful decision. But I also realized that they were parenting in a different time and with a different style. I had to trust that they had done the best they could at that time.

It was time to forgive my parents. As an adult I didn't want to carry around my childhood anger. Even if Scamper and Mikey had remained at our house long ago, they would, after all these years, be "two dead dogs." Finally, I was able to use my own understanding of their decision to make peace with myself and my image of my parents as mother and father.

None of us is a perfect parent—is there any such thing? Bruno Bettelheim encourages us to think of ourselves as "good-enough parents," concentrating on our strengths rather than on our weaknesses. I hope my own children will remember the way I loved them, sharing with them old movies, great literature, and care for the earth and its creatures. I hope they will look on me with the eyes of love and see that occasionally I was Jesus to them, rather than remember the times I lost my temper, said the wrong thing, or acted in ways other than in their best interests.

As parents, we may never give exactly the way God gives. But we are called to share of ourselves as purely in love as we can, knowing that there will be times when our children find our love inadequate. Jesus said,

*Is there anyone among you who, if your child asks for bread,
will give a stone? Or if the child asks for a fish, will give a
snake? If you then, who are evil, know how to give good gifts
to your children, how much more will [God] in heaven give
good things to those who ask!*
—Matthew 7:9-11, NRSV

I will keep that hand-scrawled card to my father. Its accusing
"and 2 dead dogs" reminds me that I am the one in need of
forgiveness. We all are. As I share family life with Larry, Trinity,
and Justus, I will continue to look for symbols of forgiveness that
remind us all of the new beginnings we need.

Trusting in God

*P*riorities clarify during a tornado warning. One minute our family was snug in a motel room, listening to a Texas storm rage outside as we got ready for bed. The next moment we heard a pounding on our motel door.

"Tornado warning! Best get to the office for further information."

We tried to move hastily without alarming our young children. Larry and I grabbed the essentials for tornado survival with a three and a half year old and seven month old: extra diapers, changes of clothes, sweaters, Cheerios, a Bible, *Frog and Toad Are Friends,* and Trinity's beloved dolls, Sojourner Truth and Lucretia Mott.

"Aren't we going to bed?" Trinity asked, confused that her routine had been shaken.

"We'll go to bed a little later tonight, honey," I responded cheerfully. "Right now, we're going to the motel office to find out what's happening with the storm."

I could feel the fear on my face—big eyes, tight lips, watchful—as Larry and I carried our children to the motel office. Many other travelers were gathered there in the hallway, but certainly not all who were staying at the motel. How could anyone feel nonchalant about a tornado? I had visions from the movies I had seen that featured tornadoes—*The Wizard of Oz, Places in the Heart*—did this motel have a storm cellar?

We waited, crowded in the hallway because there was no storm cellar. With all the glass in the building, I would have felt safer in our own cozy rented room, but I heeded the manager's request that we stay close for further information. Outside the storm continued, magnificent and terrifying in its power. Some hardy souls ventured out every few minutes to watch the sky's dark activity—was a twister coming?

Trinity sat on Larry's lap, listening to him read of the beautiful friendship of Frog and Toad. Cradling Justus against me, I talked with a woman who was in Texas for the Southern Baptist Convention. She had lived through many tornadoes, including one that had destroyed her town in 1979. She was wary and nervous.

I looked at Justus, attempting to memorize every detail of his sweet face. I held my son tight. He was too young to die. My fear escalated. Every muscle in my body tensed with terror at the thought of Justus and Trinity losing their young lives.

The fear welled up and my stomach tightened. Then suddenly, with the rain pelting against the roof, I heard the whisper of a hymn come from somewhere deep inside myself.

We've come this far by faith,
leaning on the Lord.
Trusting in God's holy word—
God's never failed us yet.

This was not a hymn I had grown up singing, but it was nevertheless inside me, singing *to* me over and over, until I had to stand up and sing softly to myself while rocking Justus. Singing so only Justus could hear, I repeated "God's never failed us yet" again and again. My breathing slowed, and the adrenalin that had been surging through my bloodstream eased into relaxation.

Trinity chortled at a joke from the book. Lucretia Mott and Sojourner Truth also sat on Larry's crossed legs, their facial expressions unchanging as they too listened to the story. Justus and I joined them on the floor and snuggled in close, concentrating on the book rather than the storm. I was no longer afraid and in panic-mode. The rain was not a monster at the door because "we've come this far by faith."

Faith is the road . . . the journey . . . the destination.

The motel manager passed through the crowd.

"Y'all can go back to your rooms now. Tornado seems to have gone about fifteen miles north." No further explanation; the storm was past.

This was not the first time, nor the last, that my fears were calmed by words of scripture or a verse from a hymn. Even when I have not been able to pray, God has somehow spoken to me in a way I could understand.

> *Those who trust in the Lord are like Mount Zion, which cannot be moved, but abides forever. As the mountains surround Jerusalem, so the Lord surrounds [the] people, from this time on and forevermore.*
>
> —Psalm 125:1-2

I wish I could say that I am always as steadfast as Mount Zion. Many times, however, this is not the case. Many times I am a frightened child inside, even though I try to give the appearance of a confident adult. The fear never consumes me, though. God always comes to sit with me until my anxiety subsides and I realize once again that God is in charge.

When my children experience fear, anxiety, or a crisis of confidence, I encourage them to take those feelings to God. I tell them of times when I have been afraid or ill at ease. We sometimes look at people in the Bible who have gone through fear to faith. We may sing a song like "Through it all, . . . I've learned to trust in Jesus, I've learned to trust in God."

Fear is a normal human emotion that we can experience without embarrassment or shame. When we are able to share our fear with God, we sometimes come "through to the other side," where we can live in trust despite situations that may cause us to be afraid or lack confidence.

We read in 2 Corinthians 5:7, "We walk by faith, not by sight." When my mother was diagnosed with inoperable cancer of the bile duct, none of us knew what her dying would be like—for her or for us as a family. Her faith-filled acceptance of the situation set a tone for us so that we were able to walk with her through those difficult weeks, mindful of our feelings but not overcome by anger, fear, or sadness.

"There comes a time in every human life when medical science can do no more for the body. I am sorry to tell you, Wanda, that you are at the point where we can do no more for you." The doctor's eyes filled with tears as he stood beside Mom's hospital bed. "We will do everything in our power to make you comfortable. I promise you that."

Until the previous week, we had all considered my mother to be a healthy woman—active in church and volunteer organizations, an avid camper and birdwatcher. The tumor in her bile duct had probably been growing silently for six months. We had no clues as to its insidious existence until the day after her seventy-second birthday, when she was hospitalized with extreme jaundice. Now we stood around her hospital bed— doctor, husband, son, daughter—all wordless in our pain.

My mother remained calm, reaching out to take the doctor's hand. "I know you have really tried and done your best with me. I so appreciate all your care." There was no denial of her condition, only gracious acceptance.

After the doctor left, my father, brother, and I stood in silence only briefly before my brother, Bill, said—in response to an earlier joke about her good appetite and the dinner she'd been enjoying—"Well, Mom, you'd better finish your tapioca pudding."

Courage takes many forms. I saw my mother's courage when she picked up her spoon and began to eat tapioca pudding immediately after being told she would soon die. If she had cried, we would all have broken down, and that would have been okay. As it was, we quietly talked a few more minutes before Dad and Bill left.

I stayed longer with Mom. I was not her pastor, but none of her ministers were there at that crucial moment. What might she need from me now?

My mother, spoon in hand, smiled wanly at me. "I'm so glad I was raised in a Christian home. God has been with me through all my life, and my faith in God is strong."

Another hymn comes to mind: "I will trust in the Lord . . . 'til I die." I wondered at how Mom could be so serene in the face of such news. Her faith held her together. During the next seven weeks, my mother's faith held all of us together. The promise of the resurrection was not just words on paper. We could make it through her all-too-sudden dying because we trusted that God's strength would carry her through this final illness and into the next life.

"Are you praying for a miracle?" someone asked me.

"No," I answered, somewhat surprised by my own response. "I think we're already seeing a miracle in the way my mother is facing her death. It is a miracle that we are all getting to spend so much time together, sharing love while she is still alive."

Trinity and Justus were very much a part of this process of transition. From the start, they knew and understood the diagnosis and prognosis. They took their cue from their grandmother, however, and the other adults around them. We talked a lot about how the illness affected us and what this meant for our future. Both children seemed to know that, because God had been faithful in the little things, we could trust that God would see us through this "biggie" of a grandmother's dying. Sure enough, we were sustained by God and the community of faith, even when the pain of her death threatened to overwhelm us.

Trusting in God means expecting the best—not the worst—of life in all its possibilities. This came home to Justus one day when he was lying in bed, fighting the fact that he had to get up and go to school.

"I know I'll have a bad day," Justus grumbled. "I just know it."

I rubbed his back. "How can you be so sure?"

"Because I often have a bad day." Conclusive evidence, his tone of voice implied.

"Is your whole day bad?"

"No," he grudgingly admitted. "There are lots of good parts, but it's easier to remember the bad parts." I was glad that he at least realized that his perceptions were shaped by memory, as well as by reality.

I drew an invisible picture on the wall with my finger. "Pretend this is a glass," I said. I then drew a line across the imaginary glass. "If there is water up to this level, is the glass half-empty or half-full?"

"Half-empty," he said assuredly. (At least he was consistent!)

I then explained the concept of how the way we view a particular situation influences how we experience it. If we view life as half-empty, we will see more of the negative side, not letting ourselves see the positive; if we see life as half-full, we are more likely to look for the good and be glad we're alive. Two people viewing the same situation might perceive it as being fortunate or dreadful, depending on how they look at it. I encouraged Justus to try to see things as half-full, rather than half-empty.

Justus was soon up and ready to go, but I didn't feel that he had really understood my point. "So much for *that* object lesson," I thought to myself.

As we drove to school, I asked him, "Did you kind of get the difference between half-full and half-empty?"

"I think so." He paused to reflect. "Does it mean that I can make a difference in my day if I have a good attitude?"

"Exactly!" Wonder of wonders, our conversation had made sense.

When I picked Justus up, I asked, as I often do, "How was your day at school?"

"Kinda half-empty in the morning, I guess; but by lunchtime I was able to see things more half-full." He considered. "A pretty good day, actually."

Jesus said, "I came that they might have life, and have it abundantly" (John 10:10). He didn't say, "I came so they would never know heartache or poverty or misunderstanding or depression. I came so they would get everything they wanted from life, have no difficult decisions to make, and live free of conflicts."

Trusting in God means living expectant of the good that God has in store for us. Yes, there will be moments when we are ready to pack it in and never get out of bed. There will be moments when we are afraid and confused, unsure of which path to take. The good news is that we have Someone who will walk with us through the fear, confusion, and new directions.

> *Who will separate us from the love of Christ? Will hardship, or distress, or persecution, or famine, or nakedness, or peril, or sword? . . . No, in all these things we are more than conquerors through him who loved us. For I am convinced that neither death, nor life, nor angels, nor rulers, nor things present, nor things to come, nor powers, nor height, nor depth, nor anything else in all creation, will be able to separate us from the love of God in Jesus Christ our Lord.*
>
> —Romans 8:35, 37-39

Bearing One Another's Burdens

*T*he young widow sat in my office, sobbing into a tissue. I had performed Rosalie's wedding only months earlier; now her husband was dead of a stroke at an early age. I sat in my chair, trying to decide whether to go over to Rosalie and wrap her in my arms so she could really cry or simply to listen as she talked her way to calmness.

Just then, Trinity looked up from where she sat playing. Nine months old, she spent her days with me at the church where I served. My office also functioned as a nursery, with its crib, rocking chair, toys, and diaper bag. Trinity looked at Rosalie, who was now left alone at twenty-one with a baby on the way. She cocked her head, first one way, then the other. Then, decisively, Trinity began to crawl toward her.

"Oh, no," I thought. "Is Trinity going to disturb Rosalie?" I was sensitive to the fact that some people consider a baby in the workplace to be an intrusion, but I watched as my daughter made her way across the room. When she reached Rosalie's chair, Trinity came to a halt and pulled herself to a standing position, looking intently at the grieving widow. She then gently patted Rosalie's knee, her tiny hand going up and down, up and down.

111

"I know," Rosalie snuffled, attempting a smile. "It'll be all right."

I sat, mesmerized. This toddler had somehow recognized an adult's need and met it instinctively. Through a nonverbal communication, Trinity had reached a hurting person more quickly than I as a counselor might have done.

Since Justus and Trinity have been so much a part of our parish ministries, they learned early on that there were times when they had to share their parents with other people who were needy in a variety of ways. In the long run, the clergy family comes first; but there are times when the needs of others prevail upon the minister, causing the family to have to wait (as is the case in families of doctors and others in helping professions). When someone is rushed to the hospital, dies, or has a nervous breakdown, that need is immediate and crucial.

Many clergy children grow up learning to put the needs of others before their own. This helps them develop into compassionate people; but I have known of parsonage children who felt abandoned and unvalued by their clergy parents. It is a fine balance to enable the "P.K." (preacher's kid) to feel important in the family, while he or she understands that others' needs may occasionally take priority. I often felt pulled while serving a church during Trinity's first three years.

"Trinity, I really want to stay and play with you like we'd planned, but Lela just called, and they're taking Louis to the hospital. They need me with them right now because they're scared. So I'm going to the hospital while you stay with Dad. I'll see you later. I love you." Because Trinity had been with me numerous times to visit Louis and Lela, she seemed to think that was okay.

This did not always feel okay to *me*, however. Larry and I have decided to serve as copastors of the same church for the past eight years so that one of us can always be available to our children. I think my children deserve to have their needs met as much as any parishioner. Sharing a ministry at a small-membership church has enabled us to be with our children most of the hours they are not in school. As much as possible, the after-school time is kid-oriented, with one parent spending time with the children. This usually means we do churchwork at the office or at home late in the evenings, after Justus and Trinity have gone to sleep.

Because church ministry can easily encroach on family time, we have learned to set boundaries to protect our family time. This came home clearly to me one evening when someone called while I was helping Justus with homework. The intensity of this person's need caused me to physically turn away from my son so I could focus on the person crying at the other end of the phone.

"Mom, I don't know how to do this. I need help," Justus said quietly. I was having a hard time concentrating on the phone conversation, and felt slightly resentful of the caller. This *was* Justus's time. I shook my head at my son, however, as he repeated his request. Finally I put my hand in front of my face: "Go away!" I hissed. I was instantly sorry that I was not available to Justus. The person on the other end did not have a pressing need. But now she poured out her heart for half an hour, while Justus waited for a simple answer to his question.

It was then that I determined that I could not live stretched and pulled in this way. We bought an answering machine, telling people that if they wanted to talk to us, they should call after eight in the evening. "From five to eight is our family time. If you

113

call then, you are likely to get the answering machine. Leave a message, and we will call you back after eight o'clock." This enables us to concentrate on homework, dinner, and bedtime rituals without interruptions. It also models to our congregation a way for families to make time to be together.

Parents must set their limits and find what works for their family. I knew that I did not want to live with my hand between my child and myself, hissing, "Go away!"

The question for any Christian is how to find a balance between giving of oneself for others and giving oneself away. This question is not just an adult one. Now that Justus and Trinity are elementary-school age, they are working out for themselves what it means to live cognizant of others' needs while also aware of their own requirements for wholeness. I am pleased when they are self-giving; I am also proud when they know when to say no. I want them to be like Jesus who was moved to compassion when he saw the crowds but also knew when to withdraw to a quiet place to be alone and pray.

Trinity and Justus are growing up in a laboratory of love—not just hearing about God but knowing that God works in specific situations with specific people. Two of those people are their parents, who work as ministers in a local congregation. Justus and Trinity also witness and participate in ministry at church, home, and school.

With two ministers for parents, our children witness the pain of broken relationships, struggles with addictions, poor self-esteem, and spiritual crises. They also see broken lives put back together in amazing ways. The recovering drug addict reaches yet another milestone in sobriety, and her pride is visible. The abused child realizes it was not his fault and begins to smile. Someone who first came to our church with a limp-fish handshake, devoid of confidence, now reaches out to give big hugs, feeling loved and accepted.

While we do not share inappropriate details of our counselees' lives with our children, we do try to help them look with love at hurting people.

"We need to be patient with (another child) right now. His parents are having a hard time communicating with each other. It must be very confusing to him to hear so much anger at his house." "She seems irritable to you? Well, let's pray that she finds the peace she seems to need."

When my children come home from school with tales of a class bully, whiner, or snob, I try to hear their feelings, even as I remind them of the other child's feelings. "Something may be happening at home that makes him or her act out at school. Is there anything you can do to be a friend?"

I was touched one day when Justus spoke of a boy he has felt to be mean and bullying. "I feel sorry for him, Mom."

"Why?"

"Because he's had such a hard time with his parents' divorce—I can tell he's angry—and now he is in a grouchy teacher's class. More than anybody, he needed a nice teacher."

I thought of Zechariah's prophecy about Jesus as the one who would "give light to those who sit in darkness and in the shadow of death, to guide our feet into the way of peace" (Luke 1:79). Giving light begins with taking time to understand another's stage of life—hurts, celebrations, confusions, clarity.

Sometimes I wonder if seeing so much suffering in lives around them is overwhelming for such young persons. Yet our children also see people overcome the odds with the help of God and

God's people. These people make it through grieving, betrayal, woundedness to come out whole on the other side.

> *We who are strong in the faith ought to help the weak to carry their burdens. We should not please ourselves. Instead, we should all please our brothers [and sisters] for their own good, in order to build them up in the faith.*
>
> —Romans 15:1-2, TEV

One young mother we know has, because of personal problems, at times been impatient. When her tolerance for her child's behavior disappears, something in her seems to snap. She often roughly grabs the child and marches away from whatever has caused the blowup. Trinity had noticed this pattern for some time. One day she decided to change things.

The child became whiny, the mother impatient. We could hear the whispered threats and see the glowering look. Before the usual pattern was complete, Trinity went over and asked, "Can I hold her?" The youngster's face relaxed; she felt special to get attention from a "big" ten year old. She began to laugh and sing a silly song as Trinity walked with her.

"When I saw my daughter with Trinity, I realized how stressed-out I was. Those few minutes of relief made all the difference. I took some deep breaths and realized that though my daughter had been getting on my nerves, what she was doing was not really a big deal. I was ready to take her back after a while and didn't feel mad at her anymore."

Trinity's caregiving to this young mother and child came as instinctively as did her crawling over to the young widow years before. Compassion cannot be forced; concern for another must come from a strong sense of self as well as a loving openness to the needs of others.

Both of our children have developed into helpers at the church nursery school. Since they are around so many little children, they are sensitive to preschooler needs.

"Mom," Justus came to tell me one day. "I'm worried because there's a ladder leaning against the roof where someone was working. What if one of the little kids like Andrew gets out and climbs up on the roof?" We made sure the ladder was moved, thankful for Justus's observant eye.

One day, late in the afternoon, Trinity was waiting at church for Larry to finish his office work. The assistant director of our nursery school asked her to do a favor.

"Will you put away all the bikes for me, Trinity?" Teresa asked. Trinity walked around the large playground, rounding up an assortment of bicycles and wheeling each one to the storage shed. Teresa, tired at the end of a long day, continued to care for the children who had not yet been picked up. When the last child had gone home, Teresa wearily went out to the parking lot and found a note tucked under her windshield. What she read lifted her spirits:

> Teresa,
>
> Thank you for letting me put the bikes away. It helped me get closer to God. I like the feeling I get when I go the extra mile.
>
> Thanks agian [sic],
> Trinity Peacock-Broyles

"Here I thought I was imposing on Trinity by asking her to do this job," Teresa said. She turned it around and made it seem like I had given *her* a gift."

We never know when our actions will influence another person in a positive way. I know that many times my children minister to me, lifting my spirits and giving me strength to meet parishioners' needs. Justus likes to give special drawings to Larry and me. Trinity leaves notes for us in unexpected places—such as on the grocery list where, along with "cat litter," "carrots," and "milk," she wrote, "Your [sic] the best parents a kid could ever have."

"Be alert, stand firm in the faith, be brave, be strong. Do all your work in love" (1 Cor. 16:13-14, TEV). Paul also writes, "Bear one another's burdens, and in this way you will fulfill the law of Christ" (Gal. 6:2). Our family is learning how our time together as a foursome undergirds each of us. We then can reach out to others whose needs don't always come at convenient times.

There are instances when, like Jesus, we need time away to pray, to think, and to just be together and enjoy each other's company. That is part of bearing each other's burdens within our own family unit. Other times we can be available to others' needs, putting our family time second, bearing the burdens outside of our immediate family.

There are times when push comes to shove, and I feel caught between my own family's needs and the needs of others. There are also wonderful moments, however, when I see a depth of compassion in my children that makes me know that they are learning important lessons about "do all your work in love."

One day, a church member's young son locked her keys in her car. She called for assistance and, when we left for home, was waiting for a road service to come help her. As we were having lunch, Justus said, "Can't we call Karen? I want to make sure she got home okay." Of course we called, and Karen was moved to know that a young friend had continued to be concerned about her.

Trinity answered the phone one night and came to me with serious face. She told me who was on the line waiting to talk to me, then added, "She sounds upset. I know it'll help her to talk to you, Mom, so take your time."

"Beloved, let us love one another, because love is from God; everyone who loves is born of God and knows God. . . . those who love God must love their brothers and sisters also" (1 John 4:7, 21). Keeping these words in mind, we all learn and grow in a laboratory of love.

Learning Our Limits

We did not know his name until he was dying in front of us, convulsing under frantic CPR efforts to revive him. We had not expected death that day. In fact, we had felt full of life and possibility as we boarded the boat at Fitzroy Island for a morning of snorkeling at Little Fitzroy Island. We learned too much of death that day and came face to face with our own human limitations.

For our family, five weeks in New Zealand and Australia were a dream vacation. On Fitzroy Island, we experienced the wonder of the Great Barrier Reef and got our first taste of snorkeling among the multicolored coral and fish in warm, ultramarine waters. Our days on Fitzroy had been relaxed—following "Wonga" the kangaroo as she hopped around the island, hiking up to the island lighthouse, swimming in the ocean.

There had been two difficult moments for me, however. Our first day there, Trinity (then eight years old) had wanted to swim to a huge floating dock out past where the waves broke. Trinity's continual desire to try new adventures always awes me. Though I was fairly adventurous as a young person, I find myself growing more cautious as I get older. Even though it looked a long way out, and I had no personal inclination to swim to the dock, I swam next to my daughter, wanting her to have a positive role model of a strong, capable woman.

Once we had climbed the ladder to the dock, I knew I had made a mistake. I absolutely hated being on the dock. It felt like we were two stories above the ocean. Trinity, ever brave, promptly dove off the dock, climbed back up the ladder, and dove again and again into the brine. I did well to stay calm as I lay on the dock's wet surface, trying not to think how deep the ocean was.

Trinity was soon ready to go back to shore. She dove off again and blithely swam toward the island. I looked over the edge of the dock, panic settling in my chest as a fearful voice residing deep inside me said, "*You* can't jump that far!" I felt paralyzed as I sat on the dock's edge, feet hanging over, body stiff and immobile. Trinity reached the shore, looked back, and waved to me. "Come on, Mom!"

I pictured myself requiring a rescue team to pry me off the dock's heights. After what seemed like an eternity of trying to talk myself into jumping, I finally moved with caution and timidity down the ladder to make my jump as short as possible. Somehow my arms propelled me back to the island but my fears were not entirely conquered.

Our resort provided canoes for our use, and, of course, both children were eager to ride around the island. As each canoe held two people, the obvious solution was that one parent pilot each canoe with one child as passenger. Given a history of having once almost drowned in Denmark, along with the fact that there were no lifejackets and the recent memory of my fear on the floating dock, I was not ready to climb into a canoe and paddle into the ocean.

"Since I don't know lifesaving, I don't feel comfortable taking responsibility for one of you kids in the ocean," I explained. "For Dad, it's different. He's a strong, confident swimmer and has taken lifesaving. For me, that feels like too much."

Despite the children's protests, I held to my decision, feeling very much the "Cowardly Lion" but unwilling to put my son's or daughter's life in jeopardy. I was daunted by my limitations. So, two days later when we decided to go to Little Fitzroy island to snorkel, I went—fearfully, but determined to give it a try for my own sake as well as the children's.

Thirteen of us climbed into the small boat and chatted amiably amongst ourselves as Steve, the driver, took us around the island to the smaller isle. Steve gave us a brief safety talk about how to handle the ocean and what signals to give if in distress. "Stay with your partner," he cautioned, as we set out to explore and snorkel.

Looking out of the open-sided boat, I felt overwhelmed by the size of the waves and the depth of the water. My eyes met Justus's gaze; his fear matched my own. "Shall we sit a minute until we feel ready?" I asked. He nodded gratefully. Trinity and Larry, on the other hand, were the first people out of the boat, diving into the water in search of exotic coral formations.

Almost immediately, however, Trinity was back on the boat, along with two of the adults who had jumped in. "The waves are just too big for me," she said in disappointment.

"I'll take us to a quieter place," Steve said, turning the boat around.

I tried to keep Larry in sight. He was the only one snorkeling by himself, in what looked like a very big ocean. We had barely turned the boat around and started in another direction when a young woman who had come back on board said evenly, "Looks like we'd better go back. My brother-in-law needs help."

Someone was clearly in distress; his partner struggled with him in the water, trying to hold him up or calm him. I saw Larry swim toward the pair; he must have heard their cries.

I quickly moved myself, the children, and our things to the side of the small boat. The young man was quickly pulled aboard, an effort requiring several adults. He was not conscious. They laid him in the flat midsection of the boat and began CPR efforts.

"I do not want you to watch this—absolutely!" I told my daughter and son, gathering them close to me and turning their heads out toward the sea. "I'll explain everything to you later." Absolute silence was broken only by the calm voices, repeating, "Breathe, Michael, breathe! Come on, Michael. You can do it, Michael!" Trinity and Justus heard everything.

As it turned out, three doctors were onboard, including Michael's brother and sister-in-law. They used oxygen and seemed at first to expect the young man to cough and perk up. Steve quickly picked up the other snorkelers and sped the boat away from Little Fitzroy.

"He needs to get to Cairns," someone said, in a voice that chilled me. Rather than risk the half-hour boat trip to that mainland city, though, the driver chose to go back to the island and call a helicopter. We sped along, Michael convulsing and vomiting at our feet. Justus's snorkeling mask was still on top of his head; Trinity kept hers on over her face, breathing through her mouth as though to protect herself from the tragedy that unfolded literally at our feet.

I held both children against me, shielding their eyes and trying to speak calmly though I wanted to sob. "Michael seems to have swallowed too much water," I said softly. "He's getting help but we can help by praying."

I took a deep breath, then repeated over and over like a mantra, "Please, God, let Michael live. Please, God, let Michael live."

When we had boarded the boat less than an hour earlier, I had not paid much attention to Michael. The best view I'd had of him was when he was unconscious, covered with vomit, his eyes rolling. Yet I wanted nothing more in the world than that he revive and live.

Across the boat, my eyes met those of another mother, whose three year old sat nonchalantly, not comprehending the emergency in front of him. Bound by tragedy, we searched one another's faces around the boat. There was only one important thing at that moment. "Please, God, let Michael live."

Steve crash-landed the boat and ran for the island nurse. I took Trinity and Justus off the boat and stood nearby under a palm tree. "We've just been through something hard, and we're going to need to talk about this experience a lot. But right now, I still feel pretty upset, so I think I'd better wait to talk about it," I told my children, certain that I was close to breaking down. Larry stood by the boat, ready to help if needed.

The drama continued as other medical staff took turns working over Michael's body. I decided that it was probably not best for my children to stand and watch any longer so we walked away from the beach. Trinity, silent since Michael's body had been pulled onto the boat, said vehemently, "I am never going into the ocean again in my life!" It took some persuasion on my part to get the kids to even dangle their feet in the water of the resort swimming pool. I tried to restore normalcy, but as long as the battle for life continued on that small boat, all other activities seemed trivial.

The helicopter arrived fifty minutes later. Michael John Francis was declared Dead On Arrival at the Cairns hospital, only a few hours after he and his family had arrived from Wales for a vacation in Australia. An autopsy failed to discover the exact reason why this healthy young man should die so suddenly, though many of us speculated. (In the face of tragedy, don't we all search for reasons for another's fate, as if to ward off our own?) Was it connected to the fact that he ate a large meal right before going into the water? Did he panic when he saw the boat turn around and leave him behind in its search for calmer water? We'll never know. I corresponded with Michael's sister-in-law for months, having made contact with them to offer support before they left Fitzroy Island.

Our family did indeed spend considerable time the day of Michael's death and afterwards, processing our feelings about being so close to death. When Justus lay in a youth hostel room in Cairns that night, unable to sleep in the sultry tropical air, my heart nearly broke when he asked, "What if it was Dad that swallowed too much water today? He was by himself in the ocean."

I pulled my son close to me and hugged him tight. "Then our day would have been even more sad. And our lives would be quite different from now on." I felt the tears stream down my face as we rocked back and forth, back and forth, on the bunk bed.

We had been close to death, and though we ourselves lived, a certain innocence was gone. Intangibly, we were changed—each of us in his or her own way. For me, Michael's death was a lesson about limits. If I had been one of the first to jump into the water, not responding to my own fears, how would *I* have reacted when the boat pulled away and left me on my own? Much as I wish I were never afraid (how ridiculous—a grown woman who thinks the water too deep and waves too big to snorkel!) in hindsight, perhaps there was wisdom in my fear.

Years earlier, I had almost drowned when I joined the crowd, swimming beyond my abilities in order to save face. As an adult, do I want to subject myself to terror in order to prove my bravery? Some people wrestle their personal demons by pushing their limits. But at what cost?

I thought of the temptation of Jesus, a story I had preached so many times that I thought I knew it backwards and forwards. But wait—what was this story saying to me *now*? "If you are the Son of God, command this stone to become a loaf of bread. . . . worship me. . . . throw yourself down from here" (Luke 4:3-9). Jesus certainly had power to do any of the actions requested by Satan. Power was not the issue, however. Jesus had no need to prove anything to the Evil One. Matter-of-factly, he replied, "One does not live by bread alone. . . . Worship the Lord your God and serve only [God]. . . . Do not put the Lord your God to the test."

Jesus was clear about his identity and why he came to earth. His was not to be a reign of mundane power and prestige. He was not to be compared to the Caesars and Herods and Pilates of the world. Rather, Jesus came out to show a new model of authority. Yes, he was God's Son but he refused Satan's challenges to prove himself.

Jesus' strength lay in his willingness to accept the limits of his earthly incarnation. As Paul wrote to the church at Philippi,

Have this mind among yourselves, which is yours in Christ Jesus, who, though he was in the form of God, did not count equality with God a thing to be grasped, but emptied himself, taking the form of a servant, being born in [human] likeness. And being found in human form he humbled himself and became obedient unto death, even death on a cross.

—Philippians 2:5-8, RSV

William Shakespeare said it differently: "To thine own self be true." I am not Jesus, though I hope I have some of his traits and practices. I am Anne Broyles, which means that I am brave and forthright about some situations and timid and afraid about others. I live within the limits of who I am. At times I may choose to push beyond my present limits, but there are also moments when I must say, even to my children, "This is who I am. I'm doing my best, and right now I do not feel ready to paddle the canoe around the island or jump overboard or bungee jump. But I will push myself to climb the thirty-two foot ladder into Balcony House at Mesa Verde or go with you to face the principal or speak out on racism."

Like Moses, Rahab, Peter, or Esther, I will have times of strength when I can do difficult things with God's help. I will also certainly have times when I must accept my limits and not berate myself. In my strength and in my weakness, I am God's child.

Believing in the Resurrection

"My puppy died," Trinity cheerfully announced to anyone and everyone who would listen. "Body in garden. Really with God."

At age two and one-third years, Trinity encountered death through the demise of a beloved pet. Her experience was positive; death was natural, not a thing to be feared. Larry and I had not originally planned our dog's death to be an educational experience. We were too wrapped up in our own personal grief as we decided how to meet our seventeen-year-old dog's needs. Yet through the wrenching experience of having our dog put to sleep, we grew along with Trinity in our understanding of the naturalness of death. Our daughter was our teacher and healer.

Alfie, a chocolate-brown hybrid of beagle and terrier, had come into my life when I was thirteen. This four-week-old pup was to play an important role in my life. During my adolescent ups and downs, Alfie had understood me when I felt no one else could. If my mother and I had a conflict, I could retreat to my room and the solace of Alfie's sympathetic brown eyes and wagging tail. Into my adult years, Alfie remained my close companion and friend. When I married at age twenty-three, this Arizona dog moved to Michigan. After ten years of sunshine and outdoor living, Alfie adapted to the rigors of snowy winters. Then, when he was thirteen years old, Alf moved back across country to

California, riding cheerfully on the front seat of a rented moving truck.

Through all these changes, Alfie remained a bright and chipper fellow sojourner along life's way. At an early age, he could climb a ladder to the rooftop and knew his commands in three languages. Alfie slowed down some as he grew older but still had many lively moments. He was fifteen years old when Trinity was born in 1981. He was curious about this new family member and adjusted to the way she took our attention away from him. For his first fifteen years, Alfie had been held, cuddled, and stroked lovingly. (My mother used to say, only partly in jest, "I wish I got half the love that dog gets.") The last two and a half years of his life, Alfie received only a few pats on the head each day as we were preoccupied in caring for our young daughter.

For Trinity, Alfie was family. She loved him with total acceptance. As Alfie grew blind, Trinity would kick open the doggie door so he could find his way in and out of the house. When, due to occasional incontinence, Alfie became an outside dog, Trinity frequently went out to visit him.

It became more and more apparent to Larry and me that Alfie was failing. He was mostly blind and deaf, his sense of smell diminished, arthritis plagued his hind legs. These alone were not reasons enough to end his life. When, in the middle of the night, we would hear anguished cries for help, it became clear that Alfie was losing his ability to cope with life.

When night descended, Alfie lost his bearings. We would find him stuck in a tomato cage in the garden or with his nose up against a wall, convinced he was trapped, when all he had to do was back up. Almost every night, we would have to go and rescue him, sometimes repeatedly. Putting him inside the kitchen only reduced the space in which he could get "lost."

Finally, after much soul-searching, we decided to have Alfie put to sleep. We set up an appointment with the vet for a Thursday at twelve, giving ourselves an hour before we were to pick up Trinity from childcare. That would be enough time, we figured, to bury Alfie in our backyard.

As I was leaving my office that day, I mentioned to my secretary the difficult task before me.

"How are you going to involve Trinity?" Denise asked. "She's smart enough to understand what's going on."

Larry and I discussed Denise's idea and realized that this would indeed be an important time to share as a family. Before we could involve her, however, we had to deal with our own grief. It was extremely difficult to hold my seventeen-year-old friend as the vet injected him. At least Alfie felt the reassurance of familiar hands and a love that lasted beyond death. We cried for a long time in the car before we were able to drive home with his lifeless body.

We placed our beloved dog on the back porch, then went to pick up Trinity. The three of us then "discovered" Alfie's body on the back porch by his doghouse. Trinity accepted our explanation that Alfie was dead "and dead means that someone doesn't move or breathe anymore. Alfie is with God now." (We felt that Trinity was too young to comprehend "being put to sleep" and didn't want her to fear her own nighttime sleep.) Our two-year-old hugged and stroked the dog, amazing us that she so naturally accepted death as part of life.

We had a simple ceremony of burial. Larry dug a deep hole by one of Alfie's favorite places in the vegetable garden. We gave thanks to God for the seventeen years this dog had spent on earth. Trinity joined in our prayers and gave Alfie a final kiss before we covered his body with dirt. She was subdued but seemed most concerned with our adult grief. During the next few days, Trinity frequently brought up the subject of Alfie's death, checking out her understanding of the situation. These interchanges were therapeutic for all of us as we talked about how much we would miss our dog.

About a week later, a woman in Larry's congregation died of leukemia. Because Jean was someone for whom Trinity had prayed every night, we immediately shared the news of her death with our child.

"Dead like Alfie?"

"Yes. Jean doesn't move or breathe anymore. She's with God."

The day of the funeral service, Trinity was at the church office with Larry. She went with him to the sanctuary where Jean's body was resting in its casket. Trinity wanted to see the body and give Jean a kiss.

Larry held her up so she could view the woman for whom she had prayed.

"Going to bury Jean in a hole in the garden?"

Trinity brushed her lips against Jean's cold cheek, then hopped down, content that her friend was well taken care of.

Trinity accepted death as a natural part of life. Her down-to-earth acceptance of death has often given me perspective when I have been overwhelmed by loss. There are times when my head has said, "Death is natural," but my own sense of loss has caused my heart to protest, seeing death as a usurper, seizing a loved one and leaving me alone.

Through all our years of burying an assortment of beloved pets in the garden, I have reminded my children that the love of God is stronger than death.

> *For I am sure that neither death, nor life, nor angels, nor principalities, nor things present, nor things to come, nor powers, nor height, nor depth, nor anything else in all creation, will be able to separate us from the love of God in Christ Jesus our Lord.*
>
> —Romans 8:38-39, RSV

When our dear cat, Playful, recently died of a rare liver condition, Trinity placed memorabilia of her life in her coffin: a favorite piece of rabbit fur, half a dog bone (to show her relationship to our dog, Paws), a green leaf to symbolize life and a brown leaf to symbolize death, a piece of silken fabric to show how silky she was, a Playmobil figure of a little girl, and a woven cross to represent the resurrection. Trinity then wrote on a white paper: "This is Playful the Cat. She came to us on August 27, 1988. She left us on November 11, 1992. She was much honored and loved." Quite formally, she listed all of our names.

"When the archeologists dig her grave up a long time from now," Trinity explained, "they'll know who she was and what she meant to us."

Justus got two pieces of wood to make a cross, upon which Trinity carved "Playful the Cat is buried here. She will always be loved!" Solemnly, we all signed our names. We dug her grave by flashlight in the front yard, then stood with our arms around one another as we gave tribute to a cat's life. We then went inside the house to read together *The Tenth Good Thing About Barney.* We knew Playful was in good hands, secure with God.

My children have always been there to remind me of the words I preach about new life and the naturalness of death. When we first heard the news that Magic Johnson was HIV-positive, I stood, shocked and unbelieving. This basketball star was not only a hometown hero; he was a fine human being I loved and respected.

"Mom," nine-year-old Trinity comforted me, "having the virus doesn't mean he's going to die. And, anyway, everyone has to die sometime. It's part of the chain of life."

I leaned against the kitchen counter, concentrating on my daughter's words. For a moment, *she* was older and wiser, reminding me of all the things I had taught her along the way.

"Maybe right now there is a baby being born who will someday be a great basketball player like Magic. That's the cycle of life. And Magic believes in God, so he won't be scared about dying."

"Right," I said, vaguely confused about this temporary reversal of roles. My daughter's words made sense and brought me comfort, even as I had offered her comfort many times before.

All my life, I have believed in the resurrection. Yet, in some ways, it wasn't until my own mother died that I knew beyond a doubt that there really *was* life after death. In the seven weeks between her diagnosis with cancer and her death, my mother prepared for her life to come. She viewed death as the entry point to a grand and glorious family reunion. She looked forward to seeing many people: her parents, brother, son, friends. My mother did not doubt that God was ready to usher her home.

"Life is a beautiful song," wrote Kim Christiansen, "and death is when you inhale so you can sing the next verse." I watched my

134

mother's weakening body and knew that when she sang the next verse, she would be unencumbered by the tumor pressing against her lungs and diaphragm. Breathing easily, she would be whole again. I could not wish her to stay on this earth in her condition.

Yet I was not ready to let her go, either. I was sometimes almost pained at how straightforward my mother was about her death.

"Frank," she told my father, "why don't you talk with a lawyer to see what you can do now to make things easier after I'm gone?"

"Anne, I want to show you the dress I want to be buried in," she said, and together we laid out the entire outfit—jewelry, shoes, and all.

We sat as a family to plan her memorial service, listening carefully to her ideas. I went through the hymnal with her as we discussed which hymns had been meaningful in her faith journey and which represented her feelings as she approached death. "Easter has always been my favorite day," she said. "Can we sing 'Christ the Lord Is Risen Today'?" Other hymns she selected included "Precious Lord, Take My Hand," "Softly and Tenderly Jesus Is Calling," and "The Lord Is My Shepherd." Thanks to my father's suggestion, we also sang "Amazing Grace," with a verse in Cherokee to affirm my mother's tribal heritage.

I sat on her bed, reading various passages from the Bible until she heard John 10:10-14: "I came that they may have life, and have it abundantly. I am the good shepherd. . . . I know my own and my own know me."

"I'd like that to be read at my service," she exclaimed. "God has shepherded me through so much."

I had been a Christian for thirty-eight years, but as I walked with my mother on her journey toward death, I leaned on God's promises in a new way. I never doubted a moment that she would be with God after her death. As I saw the effects of the cancer on her body, I was thankful that she would be made new in the resurrection.

> *The truth is that Christ has been raised from death. . . . This is how it will be when the dead are raised to life. When the body is buried, it is mortal; when raised, it will be immortal. When buried, it is ugly and weak; when raised, it will be beautiful and strong. When buried, it is a physical body; when raised, it will be a spiritual body. . . . For what is mortal must be changed into what is immortal; what will die must be changed into what cannot die.*
>
> *— 1 Corinthians 15:20, 42-44, 53, TEV*

When my father called in the early hours of January 20, 1992, I knew his news as soon as the phone jarred me from sleep. This death was expected; I knew it was imminent when I had left Tucson forty hours earlier. But those facts did not ease my pain. I sat in bed, crying, as Larry sleepily held me. We had already packed our bags and made arrangements for our church responsibilities so we could leave within two hours of the phone call.

I woke Justus.

"Honey, we've had a change of plans. Papa just called and told us that Nana died a little while ago. So now, we're leaving in an hour to drive to Tucson for the week." I stroked his cheek, urging him to wakefulness. "This is a sad time for us, but together we'll all get through it."

"Mom," Justus replied, yawning. "I'm just so glad that Nana doesn't have cancer anymore."

Trinity and Justus never did fall apart and cry after my mother died. Through her illness, they had known exactly what was happening; her death had been expected. Several weeks before, when we prepared to leave my parents' home after a Christmas visit, I told them, "This is probably the last time you will see Nana in person. So you need to say good-bye in your own way."

Justus blurted out, "Good-bye, Nana. See you in heaven."

Trinity wrote a note to be read after she had returned home:

> I will treasure the moments that I've had in my life
> with you forever. I love you very much! My dearest Nana!
> your granddaughter,
> Trinity Joy Peacock-Broyles

In my own grief, I was grateful that my children not only understood the naturalness of death but also believed their "Nana" to be alive in a different way with God. To be honest, though, there were also times when I wanted company in my misery and wondered why they weren't as outwardly emotional about her death as I. I had to learn again that each person grieves in his or her own way. My children's calm acceptance of Nana's death was no less heartfelt than my own wrenching anguish at her loss.

When my mother died, I knew deep within that she was indeed with God. I might not know or understand the specific form that life after death might take, but I know that my mother has not disappeared into nothingness. My faith, strengthened by the example of my mother and my children, is certain that the One who created us has plans for us even when we finish this earthly life.

> Soar we now where Christ has led, Alleluia!
> Following our exalted Head, Alleluia!
> Made like him, like him we rise, Alleluia!
> Ours the cross, the grave, the skies. Alleluia!

Epilogue

A very wise person once said, "Parents must give their children two gifts: roots and wings." I have found this to be true in our family life. I want my children to know the soil in which they are rooted so they may feel secure about who they are and be strong in self-esteem. I also want them to feel free to fly in new directions; not bound by the limitations others may place upon them.

I work hard to help Trinity and Justus feel secure: loved and able to love, accepted for who they are and ready to accept others, aware of their own needs and sensitive to the needs of others. I also know that they are unique individuals who may take off to uncharted spaces that are different than those I dream for them.

When Justus was an infant, a friend said to me, "Given who you are and who you would like your son to be, wouldn't it be funny if Justus grew up to play football and joined the Marines?"

"Well," I replied. "I hope that if Justus makes choices like those, I will understand."

Roots and wings. Those are also the gifts, I think, of the Christian faith. We are rooted in God who came to us in Jesus Christ. Christ is the foundation, the cornerstone, the soil in which we are planted. Because we are rooted in faith, we have wings to fly. The addicted person can take off in the direction of sobriety. The person in an abusive relationship is free to seek wholeness.

The one who doesn't think much of himself can find his unique self-worth. In Christ, we find wholeness and love.

Jesus used the image of vines and branches. "I am the vine, you are the branches. Those who abide in me and I in them bear much fruit, because apart from me you can do nothing" (John 15:5). Although this image may have spoken more clearly to Jesus' contemporaries in an agrarian society, our Savior tells us explicitly how we are to bear fruit: "This is my commandment, that you love one another as I have loved you" (John 15:12).

Love takes many forms. Indeed, we are called to love *everyone* regardless of his or her apparent lovability. We are called to show love even when we do not feel loving or lovable, when the ones we love act in ways we do not like, and when we are not sure that our love is enough.

Family life—whether the family is two people or thirteen—gives us the chance to practice love in all its possibilities. It is easy for me to love Larry, Trinity, and Justus because they are part of me, and I know them so well. It is also sometimes hard to love them because, in the intimacy of life together, we share our most unlovable parts with each other as well as the parts that are easy to love.

I sometimes look at my children in wonder: "Is this marvelous creature actually the fruit of my womb?" Other times (such as when Justus and his friends are having a burping contest) I may look at my offspring as if I had never seen them before: "These are *my* children?"

In family life, I also see *myself* as "Jekyll and Hyde." The intimacy of family life brings out the best in me (patience, creativity, loving acceptance) and also the worst (nasty remarks, nitpicking, holding grudges). Here I come face to face with the broad range of human emotions as manifested in the four of us.

As we seek to be like Jesus, our family learns to live honestly even with our negative parts. Though we know the sort of life to which Jesus calls us, sometimes our humanness overwhelms our divine inclinations. Since we live surrounded by God's love and share the same forgiving love that Jesus modeled, we look at one another with eyes of love, even when our words and actions are not as loving as we would like. We enjoy one another as parent and child, brother and sister, husband and wife, realizing how fortunate we are to be family together.

One dusky morning, as I was coming down a hill on my morning walk, I found myself praying: "God, help me to do great things today." Instantly I knew this prayer was wrong. Other words came from my heart: "God, help me to love greatly today."

Wishing to do great things would have set me up for failure as I embarked on a me-centered day. Instead of focusing on what great thing *I* could do, my revised prayer would help me to focus on how I could love others in their needs. What better place to begin than in my own laboratory of love—my family?

Those we consider to be members of our family are, for us, gifts from God. Through these everyday, ordinary relationships, we meet God. We know ourselves to be blessed by the mundane conversations and interactions, the times of working together and playing together, the meals shared, and dreams dreamed. We indeed come to know God through family life.

Activities for Families

Growing Together in Love: God Known through Family Life is a book written for parents. Since learning in families is best achieved through sharing, each chapter includes an activity page which can be used intergenerationally. These pages can be adapted for use according to the ages of the children. They may also be used in church congregations for a variety of ages.

Each activity page expands on the concepts of the corresponding chapter through a variety of activities: songs and hymns, scripture verses to share, art projects, outdoor ventures, storybook recommendations. (Books listed here are short enough to be read together in one session. Though some children may be too old to read "picture books," the books suggested have themes that reach all ages and will be a springboard for discussion. Older children may read aloud to the rest of the family. Most books should be available at your local library.) Find the songs and hymns listed in a number of sources, including *The United Methodist Hymnal* (Nashville: The United Methodist Publishing House, 1989).

Each family is unique; there is no "right" family in terms of the number of people, configuration of adults and children, style of interaction, theology. Therefore each family is likely to adapt the activities to their own needs. These pages provide a starting point by suggesting ways to come close to God through everyday relationships.

The time a family spends together sharing these activities should be positive and affirming. It is best to select times which can be relaxed and without intrusions so that family members can focus on each other. Depending on the age(s) of the child(ren), adults may need to provide structure. Even the youngest child, however, can bring gifts and leadership to the process.

Some families may choose to schedule regular family worship times. Others may schedule time to create art projects together. Still others may simply incorporate new "God songs" into their driving-in-the-car routines. God can be known and understood in a myriad of ways. These activities are designed to help each family discover where and when it most comfortably meets God.

COCREATORS WITH GOD

Activities

Theme:
Families learn and grow together in partnership, working together as a team for God's purposes.

Scripture Verses:
Genesis 1:26-31*a*
Ephesians 6:1-4

Sharing from Our Own Lives:
Name one thing you have learned from each family member.
When I create something, how do I feel about myself?
How do I feel toward what I have created?
How do we "create" family?

Songs and Hymns:
"All Creatures of Our God and King"
(An older child or adult can read the verses and all join in on the chorus)
"Morning Has Broken"
"All Things Bright and Beautiful"

Creating Together:
Let each person use clay, Playdough, or pipe cleaners to make a model of the family as she or he sees it. Play some instrumental music while you work and try to work in silence as each person concentrates on his or her own project. When everyone has finished, listen as each person tells how his or her creation depicts the family.

Or, use paper and paints to illustrate the creation story. Each artist should give the work a title ("And God saw that it was good" or "People come to the earth"). Then share about the work.

Supplies: clay, Playdough, or pipe cleaners, or: paper, paints, paintbrushes, and water.

Reading Together:

God's Creation—My World by Regine Schindler (Abingdon, 1982)

Ceremony—In the Circle of Life by White Deer of Autumn (Milwaukee: Raintree/Steck-Vaughn Publishers, A Carnival Press Book, 1983)

Ongoing Activities:

Try a "family meeting." Select one person to chair each meeting. (This is not just a "grownup" job.) Begin and end each meeting with prayer. Place items on the agenda and discuss each concern until resolution has been reached. Emphasize careful listening and loving response to each person who shares. Consider making family meetings an ongoing part of your life together.

KNOWN BY GOD

Activities

Theme:

God knows us as no one else knows us and loves us as only God can love.

Scripture Verses:

Psalm 139:13-14

Ephesians 3:14-19

John 4:1-39

Sharing from Our Own Lives:

Who knows you better than anyone else?

What kinds of things can God know about you that no one else can know?

If you were to sit down with Jesus, what kinds of things would you talk about?

Songs and Hymns:

"Jesus Loves Me"

"Because He Lives"

"Precious Lord, Take My Hand"

Creating Together:

Work together to write a song about how much God loves us and how well God knows us. Use a familiar tune ("London Bridge," "Three Blind Mice," "Row, Row, Row Your Boat") or make up new verses to add to "Jesus Loves Me."

Reading Together:

In the Beginning . . . There Was No Sky by Walter Wangerin, Jr. (Nashville: Thomas Nelson, 1986)

Runaway Bunny by Margaret Wise Brown (NY: HarperCollins Children's Books, 1942)

Ongoing Activities:

Encourage each family member to keep a journal in which to write or draw times when he or she feels especially loved by God. Younger children can use artwork; older children and adults can use written language as well. The journal can become a place to explore issues of faith as well as to give praise and thanksgiving for God's care.

APPRECIATING GOD'S GOOD GIFTS

Activities

Theme:

As individuals and as families, we can take time each day to "give thanks to the God of heaven, for [God's] steadfast love endures for ever" (Psalm 136:26).

Scripture Verses:

James 1:17

2 Corinthians 9:6-15

Sharing from Our Own Lives:

For what are we thankful?

How can we show our thanks?

Tell about a time when you felt especially thankful for God's good gifts.

Songs and Hymns:

"Thank you, Lord"

"God of the Sparrow God of the Whale"

"For the Beauty of the Earth"

Adult/older children can read verses; younger children join in on the chorus.

Creating Together:

Make a "Thankfulness Tree." Hike together around the neighborhood to find a suitable branch for your tree (12"–18" in length, with a variety of smaller branches coming out from it). Place it in a bowl with rocks and sand to hold it up, or use a margarine container filled with plaster of Paris to make a permanent stand. Use brightly-colored construction paper to cut out small shapes on which each family member can list one thing for which he or she is thankful. Stick each paper on a branch until the "tree" is covered with reminders of the many things for which your family is thankful.

Supplies: a tree branch, bowl with rocks/sand or plastic container with plaster of Paris, construction paper, scissors, marker or pen.

Reading Together:

The Way to Start a Day by Byrd Baylor (New York: Books for Young Readers, Charles Scribner's Sons, 1978)

I Sing for the Animals by Paul Goble (New York: Bradbury Press, 1991)

Ongoing Activities:

Learn new table graces, add to a bedtime prayer ritual, make up your own family tradition (such as the family date book/calendar). What activities will enhance your family's expressions of gratitude?

THE POWER OF PRAYER

Activities

Theme:

Through prayer, we can connect with the God who is with us in all parts of our lives. Prayer is powerful—a reminder that we are never alone. We are connected to God and others through prayer.

Scripture Verses:

Ephesians 6:18

Psalm 85:5

Psalm 4:1

Sharing from Our Own Lives:

In your own words, tell the story of how a breath prayer helped Justus adjust to first grade. Then ask the following questions:

• How do you think Justus felt before he had a breath prayer? after?

• Is there a situation in your life in which you might be able to use a breath prayer?

• When do you pray?

• Are there special occasions or times which call you to prayer?

• How do you feel after you pray?

• What things do you find hardest to pray about?

Songs and Hymns:

"Every Time I Feel the Spirit"

"Standing in the Need of Prayer"

"Kum Ba Yah"

"Let It Breathe on Me"

Creating Together:

Use a square box or large coffee can to make a container for prayer requests. The top of the box or can should have an opening into which can be put slips of paper listing prayer needs (for family members and others). At a family prayer time, each person can reach into the container and take out a prayer request. Decorate your container with a collage of pictures to show persons who might need God's love.

Or, set up a prayer bulletin board. On this board, pin newspaper pictures of world needs, photos of friends who need special prayers, and words and names to remind you of prayer concerns.

Supplies: box or can, magazines, glue, paper or bulletin board and pins.

Reading Together:

What Is God? by Etan Boritzer (Willowdale, ONT, Canada Ltd. Firefly Books, 1990)

Ongoing Activities:

Each family member can make up his or her own breath prayer. One way to do this is to think of the name you feel most comfortable using for God (Creator, Father, Mother, Lord, Divine Spirit, etc.) Then formulate a simple statement of what you need. The entire breath prayer should be only six to eight syllables and should be easy to remember. An example of this is Justus's "God, help me feel good at school."

Some people like to use a verse from a hymn ("Have thine own way, Lord," "Let peace begin with me") or scripture ("In you, my God, I trust," "Come to me and I will give you rest").

Write out each person's breath prayer so that everyone has a copy. Discuss how you can support each other through praying one another's breath prayers.

THE COMMUNITY OF FAITH

Activities

Theme:

Christian community offers us a people with whom we can share our lives and our faith in God. In community, we grow and change as we are challenged, comforted, understood, and

151

accepted.

Scripture Verses:

Ephesians 4:1-4

Philippians 2:1-5

Ruth 1:1-17

Sharing from Our Own Lives:

Who is our community?

Who are special people at church, in our neighborhood, or in our family and circle of friends who help us to know God better?

In what ways are we connected to these people?

Songs and Hymns:

"We Are the Church"

"Sweet, Sweet Spirit"

"Pass It On"

Creating Together:

Make a creation of spider web art to show how we are all connected one to another. (If you touch the spiderweb in one place, the whole web shakes.) Find an outdoor spiderless spiderweb. Place a piece of paper behind it and spray-paint the paper through the web. Carefully move the paper forward until the spiderweb sticks to the paper. Place a sheet of laminated paper on the top so you have a brightly-colored spiderweb design laminated to the paper.

Supplies: heavy construction paper, nontoxic spray paints, sheets of laminated paper.

Reading Together:

Ruth's New Family by Penny Frank (Batavia, IL: Lion Publishing, 1984)

When the Sun Rose by Barbara Helen Berger (New York: Philomel Books, 1986)

A Family Is a Circle of People Who Love You by Doris Jasinek &

Pamela Bell Ryan (Minneapolis: CompCare Publishers, 1988)
Ongoing Activities:

Do you feel your family has adequate support for who you are and what you believe? If so, schedule regular times to be with these families and friends who nurture your family. If not, think about who might become such community for you. Invite those persons or families to join you so you can get to know each other better and find ways to grow together in Christ's love.

WORKING FOR JUSTICE

Activities

Theme:

When we work for justice, we give of ourselves to help bring God's light to the darkness in our world. Whether we see immediate results or not, we can affirm with our families that we are part of God's acting for the good.

Scripture Verses:

John 1:4-5

Ephesians 5:8-9

Telling a Story:

Tell (or read) the story in the chapter about the creation of light, "Let There Be Light." Let the children act out the story of Bear, Chipmunk, and the other animals.

Sharing from Our Own Lives:

Where do we see darkness (negativity) in our world?

Where do we see light (acts of kindness, deeds of mercy)?

How are we acting as "people of the Light?"

Songs and Hymns:

"This Little Light of Mine"

"Seek Ye First"

"I Want to Walk as a Child of the Light"

Creating Together:

Make a candle centerpiece to use on your dining room table for family devotions. This can involve making paraffin candles (most craft stores have supplies and directions), or making a decorative centerpiece to hold a purchased candle. Be creative— use existing household supplies or search the yard for natural decorations such as branches, leaves, seed pods, pine cones.

Light your family candle centerpiece each evening at dinnertime and talk about the ways you have seen God's light in your day's activities.

Supplies: paraffin, wicks, forms, or a purchased candle; decorations for the candle centerpiece.

Reading Together:

The King's Fountain by Lloyd Alexander (New York: Dutton Children's Books, 1989)

"I Was There," by Marilyn Sachs in *The Big Book of Peace* (Dalton Children's Books, 1990)

The Hunter and the Animals by Tomie dePaola (New York: Holiday House, 1981)

Ongoing Activities:

Where in your community could your family be working for justice? Talk about opportunities that are appropriate. Could you help serve food at a homeless mission? collect money for UNICEF? participate in a peace march? What are some ministries of your church congregation that you can support?

RELYING ON GOD'S STRENGTH

Activities

Theme:

Inner strength and emotional security are as important as outward courage and physical strength. Relationship to God means reliance on God's strength when our own resources do not seem adequate.

Scripture Verses:

Ephesians 6:10-11, 14-18*a*

Philippians 4:13

1 Corinthians 9:23-26*a*

Sharing from Our Lives:

How are you strong?

How is God strong?

For what things do you need God's help?

In what ways are you helped with God's strength?

Songs and Hymns:

"On Eagles' Wings"

"O God Our Help in Ages Past"

"We Shall Overcome"

Creating Together:

Pantomime putting on the armor of Christ. What does it mean to wear truth? righteousness? faith? Make up a play which illustrates the strength of someone who is wearing the armor of God. How would this armor help one face an offer of drugs? an invitation to join a gang? the temptation to lie? Involve each family member and find simple props to make the play more fun.

Reading Together:

A Lion for Lewis by Rosemary Wells (New York: Dial Books for Young Readers, 1982)

Secret of the Peaceful Warrior: A Story of Courage and Love by Dam Millman (Tiburon, CA: H.J. Kramer, Inc., Starseed Press, 1991)

Ongoing Activities:

What sport or physical activity could your family do together? Plan an afternoon of soccer or basketball, frisbee, or hiking. Could your family enjoy an aerobics videotape for daily group exercise? Find ways to enjoy the strength of your bodies that are appropriate to your ages and abilities.

MAKING CHOICES

Activities

Theme:

When we understand that God is always at work in us, we are able to make choices that are healthy for us: mind, body, and spirit.

Scripture Verses:

Philippians 2:12-15
Philippians 4:8
Daniel 3:1-30

Sharing from Our Own Lives:

What are some of the choices you make each day?

Are there any especially difficult choices you face now?

What kinds of things do you consider as you make a choice?

Songs and Hymns:

"Lord, I Want to Be a Christian"

"I Have Decided to Follow Jesus"

Creating Together:

Make a collage to show some of the choices people have to make: what to buy, who to play with, what to eat, who to marry, how to treat each other, what work to do. Each person can then share his or her collage and explain why certain pictures were included.

Reading Together:

King Nebuchadnezzar's Golden Statue by Penny Frank (Batavia, IL: Lion Publishing, 1984)

Everyone Knows What a Dragon Looks Like by Jay Williams (New York: Four Winds Press, 1984)

Queen Esther by Tomie dePaola (San Francisco: Harper San Francisco, 1987)

Damien and the Island of Sickness by Kenneth Christopher (Minneapolis: Winston Press, 1979)

Ongoing Activities:

Whenever a family member has a difficult choice to make, call a special family meeting to prayerfully consider and support the one making a decision. The high school senior choosing a college, the elementary student deciding whether to try out for a play or sport, the parent wondering about changing jobs—all are concerns that can be lovingly discussed. Emphasize that the purpose of the meeting is to provide support for the choice-maker and to raise questions that might help him or her approach the decision. It is not up to the family, necessarily, to make the choice. Take some prayer time to invite God's spirit to enter into the process. End with the affirmation that "Whatever choice you make, we support you."

LIVING AS GOD'S PEOPLE

Activities

Theme:

Living as God's people means realistically assessing the world's needs, then figuring out what we as a family can do to make a difference. God's love is then acted out through us.

Scripture Verses:

James 2:14-17

James 3:17-18

Colossians 3:12-15

Sharing from Our Own Lives:

Tell the story of Justus seeing the homeless man asking for work. Ask family members to share times when they wished they could reach out to someone in need. Then tell of times when they did meet someone's needs. What is our family now doing to live as God's people? (Give yourselves credit for small acts of love.)

Songs and Hymns:

"Send Me, Lord"

"Here I Am, Lord" (chorus)

"I'm Gonna Sing" (Make up verses that apply to your discussion above: I'm gonna . . . love, serve, help, reach out etc.)

"Oh, How I Love Jesus" (chorus)

Creating Together:

Make a world map bulletin board to place in a prominent place in your home. Take map pins to designate places on the map where people you know or know of live. Either place a paper with the person's name on it with the pin or use a piece of yarn to connect between the map pin and a photo or name paper on the outside of the bulletin board. Place names of family and friends your children recognize, names of missionaries your church or denomination may sponsor, names of famous people who are doing God's work in other places (Mother Teresa, Bishop Desmond Tutu). Whenever you hear from someone who is represented on the board, look at the map as a reminder. Or if newspaper headlines mention particular places, use the map as a reference.

Supplies: world map, bulletin board (slightly larger than the world map), map pins, yarn, paper, and pen.

Reading Together:

Peacetimes by Katherine Scholes (Hill of Content Publications, 1989)

The Drinking Gourd by F.N. Monjo (Harper and Row, 1970)

People to Remember by Janaan Manternach and Carl J. Pfiefer (Paulist Press, 1987)

Ongoing Activities:

If your family has an open heart, hospitable nature, and wants to make new friends from around the world, you might consider joining Servas, an international cooperative system of hosts and travelers established to help build world peace, good will, and understanding by providing opportunities for deeper more personal contacts among people of diverse cultures and backgrounds. You do not need to have a separate guest room; sleeping bag space is acceptable. Host families provide two days of free hospitality. For more information, contact the U.S. Servas Committee, Inc., 11 John Street, Room 706, New York, NY 10038. Mennonite Your Way is a hospitality guide promoting Christian fellowship across community and denominational lines. Unlike Servas (which does not charge travelers), Mennonite Your Way asks a small donation for hospitality. For more details, write:

Mennonite Your Way, Box 1525, Salunga, PA 17538.

SYMBOLS OF FORGIVENESS

Activities

Theme:

Because we are human, there will be times in our family life when we need to ask each other for forgiveness and also to grant forgiveness to another family member. In God, we encounter love great enough to forgive any action.

Scripture Verses:

Colossians 3:13

Matthew 18:21-35

Sharing from Our Own Lives:

Tell the story of Justus flushing Trinity's bracelet down the toilet. Then ask:

- How do you think Trinity felt?
- How do you think Justus felt?
- Was making a bracelet together a good solution?
- Can you think of other ways this brother and sister could have worked out forgiveness for what happened?

Songs and Hymns:

"Jesus Loves Me"

"Freely, Freely" (chorus)

"Something Beautiful"

Creating Together:

Take a large piece of construction paper and fold it in half. On the left half, draw or paint a time when you felt the need to be forgiven. On the right side, draw or paint a time when you felt forgiven. Share your picture with other family members and tell the different feelings you had (mad, hurt, anxious) during those times. When everyone has shared, hold hands and sing together "Jesus Loves Me."

Supplies: construction paper, paints or markers.

Reading Together:

The Berenstain Bears Get in a Fight by Stan and Jan Berenstain (New York: Random House Books for Young Readers, 1982)

"The Tree House" by Lois Lowry, in *The Big Book of Peace* (Dutton Children's Books, 1990)

The Parables of Jesus by Tomie dePaola (New York: Holiday House, 1987)

Ongoing Activities:

On a three-inch by five-inch card, write the words "70 times 7" as a reminder of the time when Jesus told Peter that he should forgive his brother or sister "70 times 7" times (in other words, more times than one can count).

Role-play situations in which forgiveness in families is needed. Here are a few possibilities, or your family can make up its own role plays:

• A sister borrows her brother's baseball glove so that a group of her friends can play together. Somehow, his glove gets left at the park, and she must tell him it is lost. Characters: sister and brother.

• It's the kids' night to cook dinner. Dad says he'll be home by 6 PM. He's late and part of the dinner is overcooked. The kids worked hard on dinner and feel angry that their dad didn't let them know he'd be late. Characters: two children, father.

• A young child accidentally breaks a bottle of his or her mother's favorite perfume. Characters: young child, mother.

• A child expects a much-wanted toy as a present from Grandma, and is disappointed when she or he instead receives underwear and socks. Disappointed, the child says unkind words to the grandmother. Characters: child, grandmother.

TRUSTING IN GOD

Activities

Theme:

Trusting in God means living expectant of the good God has in store for us and, when afraid, sharing our fears with the One who walks with us through all parts of our lives.

Scripture Verses:

Romans 8:35, 37-39

Psalm 125:1-2

2 Corinthians 5:7

Psalm 23

Sharing from Our Own Lives:

Are there things about which it is hard for me to trust God?

Look at Romans 8:38-39. What are some of the things listed here that will *not* separate us from God's love?

What other things happen in our lives that, though they may seem scary or hard, do *not* separate us from God?

Songs and Hymns:

"I Will Trust in the Lord"

"God Will Take Care of You"

"Saranam, Saranam"

"We've Come This Far by Faith"

Creating Together:

Have an adult or older child read aloud Psalm 23. With oil pastels, encourage each person to draw a scene from that psalm, then paint the entire page with dark watercolor. The oil pastel picture shines through as a reminder that even when things look grim, our trust in God can shine through and keep us strong.

Supplies: watercolor/textured paper, oil pastels, dark watercolor paint, brushes, bowl with clean water.

Reading Together:

Sometimes I Get Scared by Elspeth Campbell Murray (Elgin, IL: Chariot Books, 1980)

Ongoing Activities:

At times when a family member is afraid (of a new situation, a monster under the bed, a coming event), gather together as parent/child or the total family and recite Psalm 23 together. Explain that for thousands of years, this psalm has helped God's people feel calm and secure, resting in God's love.

Part of this psalm could be used as a breath prayer:

"I will not be afraid, Lord, for you are with me."

"Surely goodness and mercy shall follow me all the days of my life."

"I will dwell in the house of the Lord forever."

"Your house will be my home as long as I live."

BEARING ONE ANOTHER'S BURDENS

Activities

Theme:

Each of us has opportunities to support other persons in times of need. When we "bear one another's burdens," we let the love of God flow through us.

Scripture Verses:

Romans 15:1-2

Galatians 6:2

1 John 4:7, 21

Sharing From Our Own Lives:

When has another person helped you? lifted your spirits?

When have you found ways to help other people?

What are possible ways to help others?

Songs and Hymns:

"Jesus' Hands Were Kind Hands"

"Jesu, Jesu"

Creating Together:

Use tempera paints to make a painting on sandpaper of people helping people. Share your paintings with each other and tell what you were thinking about.

Supplies: medium-rough sandpaper, tempera paints, paintbrushes, bowl with clean water.

Reading Together:

Brothers: A Hebrew Legend by Florence B. Freedman (New York: Harper & Row, 1985)

Now One Foot, Now the Other by Tomie dePaola (New York: G.P. Putnam's Sons, 1981)

Nobody Stole the Pie by Sonia Levitin (New York: Harcourt Brace Jovanovich, 1980)

Ongoing Activities:

Think about people you know who may need special love, attention, and support from your family. Is there a family going through a divorce? Is someone ill or depressed? Does a single mother need help with childcare? Brainstorm together about the ways your family can give that would "bear one another's burdens."

LEARNING OUR LIMITS

Activities

Theme:

Each person has strengths and weaknesses. Sometimes we choose to push ourselves beyond our present limits. Other times, we must learn about and respect the limits which may be part of our age, stage, or intrinsic makeup.

Scripture Verses:

Luke 4:1-13

Genesis 32:22-31

Sharing from Our Own Lives:

What limits do I face right now?

Are these limits permanent? or are they part of my age and stage? (For instance, most children will eventually master bike-riding and swimming. A disease, however, may be an ongoing condition.)

Are these limits I can or want to overcome?

Right now, how can I live within these limits?

How does my faith in God help me with my limits?

Songs and Hymns:

"Through It All"

"Come, O Thou Traveler Unknown"

Creating Together:

Draw a picture of your body. Use different colors to represent the parts of your body that feel strong and those that feel weak. Someone who is facing a fear might depict that fear by a blue scribble in the head; someone who feels strong of heart even though there may be other weaknesses, might draw a large red heart.

Leave your body pictures and have each family member lie comfortably on the floor and listen to soothing music for three minutes. While relaxing, each person should think of God's spirit flooding into and over his or her body. How does that spirit affect the strong and weak parts, the limitations?

Return to your pictures. Draw the image you had of God's spirit affecting your body. Then share your picture with other family members. This can be done even with very young children, but may require working as partners through the process.

Supplies: paper, markers, soothing instrumental music.

Reading Together:

All Except Sammy by Gladys Yessayan Cretan (Boston: Little, Brown, and Co., 1966)

Ongoing Activities:

Try to be aware of times when family members are facing individual limits. How can the family support a teenager who does not make the basketball team or a preschooler who is frustratedly unable (yet) to tie a shoe? A father who confronts high cholesterol or a mother who feels limited in her job? A family member who has Downs Syndrome or diabetes or a broken leg?

With someone who is feeling limitations, talk to God and picture God working in that person regardless of strengths or weaknesses.

BELIEVING IN THE RESURRECTION

Activities

Theme:

As part of life, death reminds us that the One who created us has plans for us even after we finish this earthly life. Families can use experiences of loss (a loved person or pet) to remember that God's care for us extends beyond life as we know it.

Scripture Verses:

Romans 8:37-39

1 Corinthians 15:20, 42-44, 53

Luke 24:13-35

Sharing from Our Own Lives:

What do I imagine happens after death?

What images and stories from the Bible comfort me when I think about dying?

What fears do I have about death?

In what way is Easter important to me?

Songs and Hymns:

"When We Are Living"

"He Rose"

"Christ the Lord Is Risen Today"

Creating Together:

Write a family Affirmation of Faith that includes:

• who you believe God is

• God's purpose for the world

• how God is working in life and in death

• what the resurrection means to you

• how Jesus is walking your road with you

Reading Together:

Potter: Come Fly the First of the Earth by Walter Wangerin, Jr. (Elgin, IL: Chariot Books, 1985))

Saying Goodbye to Grandma by Jane Resh Thomas (Boston: Clarion Books, 1988)

Annie and the Old One by Miska Miles (Boston: Joy Street Books, 1972)

The Two of Them by Aliki (New York: Greenwillow Books, 1979)

Ongoing Activities:

When someone close to the family is very ill and facing death, sit in a circle together as you think of that person. Hold hands and share images of how God is working in that person's life: "Imagine Grandma surrounded by the light of God's love" or "Can you see José cradled in the palm of God's hand?" Talk about how healing does not always mean physical wellness but may entail release into the Resurrection. Pray for the ill or dying person and give them over to the power of God. Affirm together that no matter what happens, this beloved person will be cared for by God.

COCREATORS WITH GOD

A Ritual for the Birth of a Child*

Thanksgiving

Sing out to God, all the earth,
Break forth and sing for joy.
Sing praises to God with the harp,
And with voices full of joyous melody.
With trumpets and the sound of horn,
Sing out to God.

Antiphon   Thank you God for the gift of birth, for love
made flesh to refresh the earth. For life and
strength and length of days, we give you
thanks and praise.

Let the sea roar in all its fullness,
The whole world and all it inhabitants.
Let the floods clap their hands,
And the mountains sing for joy
Before God and the nations. (Psalm 98)

Repeat antiphon

Hymn
"Now Thank We All Our God"

A Prayer

O God, like a mother who comforts her children, you strengthen us in our solitude, sustain, and provide for us. We come before you with gratitude for the gift of this child, for the joy which has come into this family, and the grace with which you surround all of us. As a father cares for his children, so continually look upon us with compassion and goodness. Pour out your spirit. Enable your servant to abound in love, and establish our home in holiness, through Jesus Christ, our Lord. Amen.

Naming

A name has power. It distinguishes us from another, yet connects us with our Christian roots and our family heritage.

"Fear not, for I have redeemed you. I have called you by name. You are mine. When you pass through deep waters I will be with you, your troubles will not overwhelm you. Fear not, I am with you. I have called you by name." (Adapted from Isaiah 43:1-2)

Giving of the Name

Prayer

Loving God, sustain this child with your strong and gentle care. May the life of this child be one of happiness, goodness, and wisdom. Grant that this child may seek after peace and justice, compassion and joy for all of creation.

Commitment and Wonder

Parents' Statement

> We receive this child
> from the hand of a loving Creator.
> With humility and hope
> we accept the obligation which is ours
> to love and nurture this child
> and to lead this child to Christian faith
> by our teaching and example.
> We ask for the power of the Holy Spirit
> and the support of the Church
> that we may be good stewards
> of this gift of life.

Blessing

> *(All place hands on the newborn's head)*

> From the love in the Heart of our God
> May the rising sun shine on you
> And guide your steps in the paths of peace.
> (from Luke 1:78-79)

*This service was written by Larry Peacock and used immediately after the birth of Trinity Joy Peacock-Broyles on November 14, 1981 and at the birth of Justus Simon Peacock-Broyles on September 18, 1984.

Additional Literary Resources for Families

Many books, though not specifically "religious," can bring families closer to one another and to God. In addition to the books listed on the Activities pages, the following are short books I recommend for "read aloud" time:

Baylor, Byrd, *One Small Blue Bead*. (New York: Charles Scribner's Sons Books for Young Readers, 1992.)

Bunting, Eve, *The Mother's Day Mice*. (Boston: Clarion Books, 1986.)

Buscaglia, Leo, *The Fall of Freddie the Leaf: A Story of Life for All Ages*. (Thorofare, NJ: Charles Slack, Inc., 1982.)

Cooney, Barbara, *Miss Rumphius*. (New York: Viking Penguin Children's Books, 1982.)

dePaola, Tomie, *Nana Upstairs & Nana Downstairs*. (New York: G. P. Putnam's Sons, 1973.)

dePaola, Tomie, *The Legend of the Bluebonnet*. (New York: G.P. Putnam's Sons, 1983.)

Fair, Sylvia, *The Bedspread*. (New York: Morrow Junior Books, 1982.)

Fisher, Lucretia, *Two Monsters: a Fable*. (Owings Mills, MD: Stemmer House Publishers, 1976.)

Forrest, Diane, *The Adventurers: Ordinary People with Special Callings*. (Winfield, B.C., Canada, and Nashville: Wood Lake Books, Inc., 1983.)

Fox, Mem, *Wilfrid Gordon McDonald Partridge*. (Brooklyn, NY: Kane/Miller Book Publishers, 1985.)

Gerstein, Mordicai, *The Mountains of Tibet*. (New York: HarperCollins Children's Books, 1987.)

Goble, Paul, *Her Seven Brothers*. (New York: Bradbury Press, 1988.)

Hoberman, Mary Ann, *A House Is a House for Me*. (New York: Viking Press Children's Books, 1978.)

Johnston, Tony, *The Quilt Story*. (New York: Grosset & Dunlap, Sandcastle Books, 1992.)

Joosse, Barbara M., *Mama, Do You Love Me?* (San Francisco: Chronicle Books, 1991.)

Kellogg, Steven, *The Island of the Skog.* (New York: Dial Books for Young Readers, 1973.)

Kesselman, Wendy, *Emma.* (New York: HarperCollins Children's Books, 1985.)

Klagsbrun, Francine, editor, *Free To Be . . You and Me.* (New York: McGraw-Hill Books, 1987.)

Lehn, Cornelia, (editor), *Peace Be With You.* (Newton, KS: Faith & Life Press, 1981.)

Lobel, Arnold, *Ming Lo Moves the Mountain.* (New York: Greenwillow Books, 1982.)

Luenn, Nancy, *The Dragon Kite.* (New York: Harcourt Brace Jovanovich, 1982.)

MacLachlan, Patricia, *Through Grandpa's Eyes.* (New York: HarperCollins Children's Books, 1971.)

Mattson, Ralph, *Mr. Slef.* (Old Tappan, NJ: Fleming H. Revell Company, 1976.)

Mason, Jerry, (editor), *The Family of Children.* (New York: Perigee Books, 1979.)

Mendez, Phil, *The Black Snowman.* (New York: Scholastic, Inc., 1989.)

Munsch, Robert, *Love You Forever.* (Willowdale, ONT, Canada: Firefly Books Ltd., 1986.)

Ormerod, Jan, *Moonlight.* (New York: Puffin Books, 1983.)

Ormerod, Jan, *Sunshine.* (New York: Puffin Books, 1984.)

Paulus, Trina, *Hope for the Flowers.* (Mahwah, NJ: Paulist Press, 1992.)

Pittman, Helena Clare, *The Gift of the Willows.* (Minneapolis: Carolrhoda Books, 1988.)

Pogrebin, Letty Cottin, (editor), *Stories for Free Children.* (New York: McGraw-Hill Book Company, 1983.)

Polacco, Patricia, *The Keeping Quilt.* (New York: Simon & Schuster, 1988.)

Porter-Gaylord, Laurel, *I Love My Mommy Because . . .* (New York: Dutton Children's Books, 1991.)

Scott Ann Herbert *On Mother's Lap.* (Boston: Clarion Books, 1992.)

Shulevitz, Uri, *The Treasure.* (New York: Farrar, Straus & Giroux, 1979.)

Silverstein, Shel, *The Giving Tree.* (New York: HarperCollins Children's Books, 1964.)

Viorst, Judith, *The Tenth Good Thing About Barney.* (New York: Atheneum Children's Books, 1971.)

Wagner, Jenny, *John Brown, Rose, and the Midnight Cat.* (New York: Puffin Books, 1980.)

Walter, Mildred Pitts, *My Mama Needs Me.* (New York: Lothrop, Lee & Shepard Books, 1983.)

Wangerin, Jr., Walter, *Thistle.* (New York: Harper & Row, 1983.)

Wheatley, Nadia, and Rawlins, Donna, *My Place.* (Brooklyn, NY: Kane/Miller Book Publishers, 1992.)

Winter, Jeanette, *Follow the Drinking Gourd.* (New York: Alfred A. Knopf, Dragonfly Books, 1992.)

Yarbrough, Camille, *Cornrows.* (New York: Coward-McCann., 1981.)

Yolen, Jane, *Owl Moon.* (New York: Philomel Books, 1987.)

Zolotow, Charlotte, *My Grandson Lew.* (HarperCollins Children's Books, 1974.)